You have multiplied, O Lord my God, Your wondrous deeds and Your thoughts toward us; none can compare with You! I will proclaim and tell of them, yet they are more than can be told.

—Psalm 40:5 (ESV)

DECEMBER 2015
WITH THANKS & APPRECIATION
TO A GOOD FRIEND —
BILL TAYLOR

Bill Miller

When GOD Stepped In

51 Encounters that Showed Me God is Real and I Can Trust in Him

BILL FISHER

LifeRich Publishing is a registered trademark of The Reader's Digest Association, Inc.

LifeRich Publishing books may be ordered through booksellers or by contacting:

LifeRich Publishing
1663 Liberty Drive
Bloomington, IN 47403
www.liferichpublishing.com
1 (888) 238-8637

Because of the dynamic nature of the Internet, any web addresses or links contained in this book may have changed since publication and may no longer be valid. The views expressed in this work are solely those of the author and do not necessarily reflect the views of the publisher, and the publisher hereby disclaims any responsibility for them.

Any people depicted in stock imagery provided by Thinkstock are models, and such images are being used for illustrative purposes only. Certain stock imagery © Thinkstock.

Scripture quotations marked NLT are taken from the *Holy Bible*, New Living Translation, copyright © 1996. Used by permission of Tyndale House Publishers, Inc., Wheaton, Illinois 60189. All rights reserved.

Scripture marked AB are taken from THE AMPLIFIED BIBLE, Old Testament copyright ©1965, 1987 by the Zondervan Corporation. The Amplified New Testament copyright ©1958, 1987 by the Lockman Foundation. Used by permission.

The Holy Bible, English Standard Version (ESV) is copyright © Crossway, a publishing ministry of Good News Publishers 1300 Crescent Street, Wheaton, Illinois 60187, USA.

Scripture quotations identified KJV and any not identified are from the King James Version of the Bible.

Scripture marked NIV are taken from the HOLY BIBLE, NEW INTERNATIONAL VERSION Copyright © 1973, 1978, 1984 International Bible Society. Used by permission of Zondervan Bible Publishers.

In the interest of privacy for those concerned, many of the names in this book have been changed.

Cover Design: Brad Lind

ISBN: 978-1-4897-0535-8 (sc)
ISBN: 978-1-4897-0537-2 (hc)
ISBN: 978-1-4897-0536-5 (e)

Library of Congress Control Number: 2015953834

Print information available on the last page.

LifeRich Publishing rev. date: 10/23/2015

I want to dedicate this book, first of all, to my dear wife, Yvonne. The fact that she was a blessing to me as my life companion for the majority of my life was due to the favor of the Lord. She has always been an inspiration to me, with her endless creative energy, her love, her support, her patience, and especially her spiritual consistency. And since she has already been summoned into the courts of the King of Kings, it is my hope and prayer that she gets word that I wrote this.

I couldn't have asked for better kids than our children, Lynn, Paul, and Anne. They have enriched our lives immensely, and now each of them is carrying the baton on the next lap around the track as good, exemplary, loving, caring parents. All along the way, as they have grown, advanced, matured, I have learned a lot from each of them. Each of them continues to enrich my life.

The grandkids! Eleven of them! Each one is unique, with an active, inquisitive, imaginative mind. I thoroughly enjoy the long one-to-one talks with them. Each one is an inspiration to me, and I continue to learn from each one of them also.

Our whole family has always been close, and that has provided a constant support and strength to all of us. And what means the most of all, now and throughout all eternity, is that I have no greater joy than to hear and be assured that my children and grandchildren are *all* walking in the truth, to slightly paraphrase 3 John 1:4.

Contents

I Shouldn't Be Alive to Write this Book...

I shouldn't be alive to write this book. I have been told by several that they are amazed that I survived the devastating auto wreck of last year. My dear wife, Yvonne, did not survive. Two of our granddaughters, also in the van, were injured. Lord, I am so thankful that their injuries were much less severe, so their athletic careers were not stopped.

During the memorial service for my wife, I stated that it had occurred to me to ask God "Why", but that I was not going to ask Him—because He had already proved Himself to me over and over again, and I trust Him.

What I was referring to was that God had already demonstrated to me His reality and trustworthiness on dozens of occasions through medically verifiable healings, through sparing me from death on several occasions, through dramatic rescues and through other encounters. Actually, I can recall no less than nine times when my life has been spared from death. My life has been punctuated with a series of miraculous acts of the Lord.

About two months later, by which time I was finally out of intensive care, was out of the hospital, and had been making very good progress in my recovery from the long list of head-to-toe internal and external injuries, I had a conversation with one of the paramedics who had been at the scene. He told me that at the time they had questioned if I would survive.

As it turned out, hospital records show that I had sustained numerous injuries which included grade three lacerations to the liver, a concussion with brain injury, a fractured collarbone, fractured rib, injuries to right arm, right ankle, both feet and both legs, as well as acute blood loss. However, recovery was progressing well.

Most have heard the expression "A cat has nine lives." The nickname of one of my granddaughters is Cat. The ironic thing is that it seems I am the one with nine lives.

I believe that God has allowed me to get into many unexpected, dangerous situations throughout my life and then has rescued me in often spectacular ways. As the memorable words say in the song "Through It All" by the gifted songwriter and musician Andrae Crouch, "If I'd never had a problem, I wouldn't know God could solve them."

However, this time it was different from all the other times. While all of the other experiences had ended favorably for me, this one time had not. While I had survived once again, nevertheless because of the sudden loss of my wife, I considered the outcome this time a disastrous loss. However I had learned through all of the previous experiences that God was real, and that I could trust in Him. So I did, and I do.

The fact that I had just been given yet *one more time* to live—to continue to live—brought to the fore the dramatic cumulative record of all the previous amazing miraculous experiences of my life—God's amazing track record.

On many occasions, when I would tell about one or another of the amazing experiences, listeners would strongly, repeatedly urge me to write a book about them. After much urging, consideration and prayer, I put pen to paper.

This is that book.

I want to say right here that I know it has *not* been because I'm in any way more special—or of any special value—to God than anyone else. I'm not—definitely not. I know that. On the contrary, I have said many times that I know God doesn't need me, but that rather I desperately need Him and desperately need to be yielded to Him.

Yet this book is *not* about me; it is about God. If it were about me, it would have a different title, such as *Undeserving at Nineteen; Undeserving Now.*

Yes, I shouldn't be alive to write this book. Nevertheless, I am here and able to write it because of the amazing mercy of God—the patient, gentle, powerful mercy of God, who has kept me alive over and over and over again. As you read, look to see God in action.

How It All Began

I had questions. Many questions. Were things today different from the way they were two thousand years ago? Even more important, does God still do what He used to do?

I came to faith at a very young age. My mother tells me that I voluntarily responded to a church altar call at the age of four. I got up from my seat and went down the aisle to the front of the church for prayer and to receive Christ as my Savior. I do not recall the occasion. I may have a vague, general memory of it, but I do not recall any specific details of that day.

I do have a few spotty memories of life at that age. I remember playing with my Tonka-size, bright-red fire truck with D-cell-battery-powered little headlights. I liked to go into our dining room after dark, turn off the lights in the room, and—down on my knees—push it around the floor under the dining room table. I have a memory of one specific time when I was told it was time to go to bed and I strenuously objected— verbally only—because it was still daylight outside! I remember a little about my first day of kindergarten, which was on Valentine's Day: the name of my teacher,

Miss Beeler; the words and music of a short song we learned that day; and the general layout of the classroom there at Hiawatha Elementary School. I also remember that Dad would read stories to me from a Bible-story book, and I can visually picture one of those times from when I was five or six and can almost hear Dad's voice.

From as far back as I can recall, I always believed the Bible. What the Bible said happened, happened. What the Bible said that God said, He said. What the Bible said that God did, He did. What the Bible said about Jesus was totally true and accurate. All the miracles recorded in the Bible—all the amazing things—did take place. I had no doubts.

I began to think about God in more depth at about age nine or ten. And then at about age twelve, I had a traumatic dream about Jesus Christ's return. The account of that dream is in the appendix in the back of this book. I knew He was real, but I had neither seen nor heard of any recent miracles or supernatural acts. I picked up the idea from somewhere that God doesn't do miracles anymore. I don't recall any specific teaching about it, but I got that idea from somewhere.

So in essence, the result for me would be that I could have said, "I know God is real in Heaven, but He's not real to me." I asked about all this, and the answer I remember was a reference to the passage in the Bible where Jesus said to Thomas, "Blessed are you, because you have seen and believe. Blessed are those who have not seen, and [yet] have believed" (Paraphrase of John 20:29). Somehow, that did not satisfy me. In fact, I was disappointed.

Eventually, in my late teens and early adult years, I began to seek out information that would provide me with verification—evidence about what the Bible said and evidence about the Bible itself. This was not because I was a skeptic. I was not a skeptic; I was a seeker.

The Bible says, "He that cometh to God must believe that He is, and that He is a rewarder of those who diligently seek Him" (Hebrews 11:6 KJV). I believed that God existed, and I had a gradually growing longing for Him to be not just real but real *to me*. Some of the essential highlights of my searching and discoveries are in the e-mail in the appendix at the back of this book.

I believe—in fulfillment of God's promise in Hebrews 11:6 together with Jeremiah 29:13–14—that He saw fit to begin to reward me for my search. That reward came to me in two ways:

1. Through the discovery of evidence, verification, and corroboration through archeological discoveries and through other valid documentation

2. Through direct, personal, verifiable, firsthand, miraculous experiences

As I think back, I believe God decided to put me into a long-range training program through which He would demonstrate to me that He is real and also active in this world—that He still performs mighty miracles today! One key byproduct of the experiences was a very gradual realization that He cares for me. Somehow, this realization was slow to sink in. I recall a conversation from back many years with my mother, when she said to me, "Billy, if you were the only person in the world, Jesus would have died for you."

I remember my answer: "Mom, I really don't think so."

"Why don't you think so?" she asked.

I replied, "Because I'm not worth it."

The realization that He cares for me gradually penetrated my skull, but somehow for me, it took a long time and many experiences. But God mercifully, lovingly, and patiently provided those experiences. I learned that He is merciful and personal and that He cares. I learned that I can trust in Him. He is real! That's what this book is about.

PART ONE

HEALINGS

1

MY VOCAL CORDS ARE RESTORED

―――――

W hat do you do for a career when you can't talk? What are your options? As a teenager, I began to wonder about that, and I hadn't come up with any good answers.

At about the time I turned nineteen, I was faced with a prolonged problem that could have changed the direction of my life unpredictably and totally. In the middle of the winter of my second year in college, I began to experience hoarseness in my voice. I had experienced hoarseness before but usually for a day or two at most and usually when connected with a cold. This was different. The hoarseness went on for weeks, and my voice became raspy. The college had an a cappella choir that went on an extended three-week tour every spring.

I had hoped to audition for a spot in the choir, but now that seemed totally out of the question. I could barely talk, let alone sing.

Several weeks passed. What could I do? What should I do? I needed answers. I went to see a specialist downtown. The doctor examined me. He said he had bad news. Due to misuse or abuse of my voice, I had developed growths, or polyps, on my vocal cords—one on each cord. He drew a sketch showing the locations of the growths. Then he brought in another doctor, who looked down my throat at the vocal cords and agreed with his diagnosis. The doctor told me that surgery was needed to remove the growths. So surgery was scheduled for a few weeks later.

Each morning during the following weeks, I would test my voice. Every morning it was the same—a raspy hoarseness with sometimes only a hiss at first. It was like that each morning until the day the surgery was scheduled to take place.

That morning. That wonderful morning. That amazing morning. That morning, when I awoke, my voice was totally clear!

When I walked into the living room, Mom was sitting in an upholstered chair with her back toward me. I stepped through the doorway into the room and said excitedly, "Mom! My voice is clear!" As I write this, emotions are welling up in me again. My gentle yet firm and characteristically calm mother, who felt things deeply—my praying mother—only said two words: "I know." She had been praying for me, and the Lord had revealed to her that He was healing me!

That afternoon, I went to have doctors look at my vocal cords. A doctor examined them and told me that

the polyps were gone. There was no longer even a trace—
no scars, no scar tissue. There was no longer any need
for surgery. He gave me good advice: to take good care
of my voice. Gladly!

A few days after that, I was talking with Jerry B.,
a fellow student and accomplished pianist preparing to
be a missionary in France. He told me that the surgery
would have been risky and delicate. A friend of his
had had the surgery, and his voice was never right. It
remained permanently hoarse and raspy. I have since
learned of other similar cases.

In the spring, I auditioned and was accepted into the
a cappella choir at the college. I began in the fall. It was
my privilege and opportunity to travel with the choir
on several tours in almost every state, and I have been
singing ever since. All this happened because of the mercy
and grace of God—and because of a praying mother. Lord,
You are so good to me, over and over again. You healed me!

This was the first of many amazing miraculous
experiences. Actually, You did two things:

- You healed me.
- You demonstrated Your reality.

"Sing to Him; yes, sing His praises. Tell
everyone about His miracles. Exult in His holy
name; O worshipers of the Lord, Rejoice!" (Psalm
105:2–3 NLT).

2

CHINA: GOD HEALS TWO IN ONE MORNING

―――――――

*L*ord, You took me halfway around the world so You could show me that You really care about me. You took me to where I had no alternatives but to depend totally on You. In a desperate situation, You showed me Your mercy, love, and care. This was the culmination of many years of struggle, uncertainty, and not knowing what to do. You healed me!

One autumn when I was an underclassman in college, my mother was driving on East River Road, north of Minneapolis, Minnesota. I was riding in the car with her. Suddenly a larger car came racing around the curve behind us and crashed into the back of our car. My mother's head struck the steering wheel, and she was dazed and unconscious for a time.

At the time, I was not aware of any personal injuries to myself. However, as time went on, I began to experience eyestrain. I needed brighter light while reading. At no time did I think that there might be a connection between the chronic eyestrain and the car accident. I went for an eye examination and was fitted with glasses, but that did not solve the problem.

I could no longer read for more than a short while in the library or under what most people would consider normal lighting without experiencing eyestrain, a serious headache, and then nausea. I found special lamps that would accommodate 150–200 watt bulbs and had to do almost all my reading in my home study area or (best of all) outside in sunlight on sunny days. A doctor prescribed Valium, but that did not solve the problem or correct my condition, so I discontinued it after a while.

Finally, after several years of struggle, a friend suggested I consult a certain chiropractor, which I did. The chiropractor X-rayed my neck and back and discovered that my neck was out of alignment in two directions: to the back and to one side. The misalignment was so serious and had been present for such a long time that it required me to return for adjustments three times per week for a few weeks, as it would slip out again. After a few weeks, I was able to reduce the frequency of visits to twice a week, then to once a week, and eventually to about twice a month. I discovered that I no longer had the eyestrain, headaches, or nausea. When I would begin to experience them again and the symptoms would begin to build over the period of a day or two, I knew to return for an adjustment.

As time went on, I continued to need to return for adjustments about twice a month. But I was free from the symptoms, and I could read almost anywhere. Then one day, I learned of an opportunity to apply to teach English at a university in China for a summer. I was interested, but I thought about my neck problem and hesitated. I spent some time praying about it. Essentially, I said to the Lord, "I don't want to go unless You go with me in Your power and protection." I went ahead and applied.

About two months later, I received word that the Chinese Department of Education had approved my application. I went through several weeks of preparation and orientation and then flew to Hong Kong for more orientation. From there I was scheduled to travel to the city of Guangzhou, or Canton, and then to board a train for a two-day ride to the north, deep into the interior of China.

The final leg of my journey was at night, about fifty kilometers (thirty miles) by van, mostly on detours on a road under construction, with lurches, jerking, and sliding —all of which could be predicted to put my neck out of alignment again. We arrived at the campus of Henan University in the city of Kaifeng at about two thirty in the morning on Saturday. Classes would begin on the following Monday.

After a few hours of sleep, I planned to spend the remainder of Saturday and Sunday getting settled and getting ready to meet classes on Monday morning. Unfortunately, I was beginning to feel the familiar symptoms gradually beginning to build, and there was nothing I could do about them. I made it through the day Saturday and went to bed to seek a good night's sleep.

I awoke on Sunday morning to beautiful sunshine and a blue sky, but the symptoms were there in my neck and head and continuing to build. I knew what was coming—eyestrain, headache, and nausea that would not stop. I began to cry out to the Lord. "Lord, I've come halfway around the world to do a job and to be a witness for You, and now I won't even be able to function." In just seconds, all the symptoms disappeared. They were gone!

About two hours later, I was outside, lying in the grass, writing about what had happened—as if I would ever forget! One of the members of my teaching team walked up and said, "LuAnn (another teacher) is having trouble with her neck. She's in serious pain." He told me that the Chinese doctor had been here but he couldn't help her. The Chinese acupuncturist had been here, but he couldn't help her either.

God had just healed me, so I said, "Let's go and see LuAnn."

As we entered the room where LuAnn was, I could see that she was in serious pain. She was sitting in a chair with her elbow on the table and her hand on the side and back of her neck, holding her head up. She was grimacing in pain. We sat down across the table from her. I asked her if I could put my hand on her neck. On the back of her neck was a prominent knot almost half the size of a ping pong ball. I asked, "LuAnn, how about if we pray?"

She began to cry. She said some of the same things I had said to God a couple of hours earlier: "I have so much to do to get ready to meet my classes tomorrow, and I can't even function." We prayed, probably not for more than three or four minutes. Suddenly, LuAnn exclaimed, "The pain is gone!" I put my hand on the back of her neck. The knot was gone!

My neck remained fine the entire time we were in China. There was no recurrence. LuAnn also remained fine for the entire time we were in China. Father God, You are so good. So merciful. So faithful. You healed two people that morning, and You set the tone for that whole summer in China!

"O Lord my God, I cried to You for help, and You have healed me" (Psalm 30:2 ESV).

3

BONE SPUR:
NOW YOU SEE IT ...

God, You have so many surprises—good surprises. Why am I always surprised when You bring another surprise?

It's amazing how important every little bone—and every large bone—is for one just to function throughout the day. One bone broken or just out of position can determine what you can or cannot do today.

One summer, while I was on staff with the college, a golf tournament was held, and I thought it would be fun to enter. The tournament was sponsored by the college, and you didn't need to be one of the greats to enter and have some real golfing fun. That suited me because, although I had played quite a lot of golf, I was not one of the great ones. Also, life had become so busy during the past few years that although I hadn't quit the game, somehow there hadn't been time for it, and it had been squeezed out and off of my calendar.

I went to the garage and got the clubs out to take a few practice swings and to begin to get in shape for the tournament (or so I hoped). A few short chip shots: okay. A few half-swings with the short irons: okay. How about a few easy swings with the driver? Ooh! That right shoulder didn't feel 'right' – (no pun intended).

My efforts to warm up and loosen up gently didn't work. I knew something was wrong, so I went to the doctor, who X-rayed the shoulder. He told me there was a bone spur that had developed on the front of my right shoulder. He showed me the X-ray, and sure enough, there it was, protruding forward.

I had three options at that point. I could either do nothing, have a surgeon go in and saw it off (my way of describing the procedure), or take pain medication as needed. Any of the three options would mean that I could not play in the tournament. I elected for option three.

Later in the year, however, I must have done something to cause the shoulder to flare up again, and I had to return to the doctor. I had apparently done something to cause muscle tissue to rub against the bone spur. The friction had caused the tissue to swell, which was painful. Unfortunately, even without motion, the passive pressure of the bone spur against the inflamed muscle tissue was very painful.

This time, the option to do nothing was no longer on the table. My options now were to be treated with cortisone (to reduce swelling of the surrounding muscle) and pain medication or to have the bone spur surgically removed. I chose the cortisone and the painkillers. The prospect of having a surgeon go into my shoulder was definitely not something that appealed to me at all, and I wasn't sure how he or she would remove the bone spur. At that point in my life, I had never been subjected to any kind of surgery, and to say the least, I was hesitant. In my way of thinking at the time, that option was off the table, at least for the present. "Maybe I might consider it later, but not now," I said.

However, the painkillers were so strong that I was pretty much groggy for the first two days of taking them. After the muscle swelling had subsided, we could reduce and then stop the pain medication. As time went on, in order to live with the problem, I learned what I could and could not do with my right arm and shoulder.

About a year later, we had moved to another state, and I decided that I wanted to solve the problem of my shoulder once and for all, even if it meant that I would have to undergo surgery. I was finally ready for surgery. I went to see a doctor in the clinic in my new city and told him of my decision and the history behind it. He X-rayed my right shoulder and came back into the room with a puzzled look.

"I don't find a bone spur on the X-ray," he said. He showed me the X-ray. I searched, but I couldn't find the bone spur either. It wasn't there. He asked me if I was sure that there had been a bone spur. I told him that there was no doubt and that it was clear and prominent on the original X-ray taken in the clinic in the other state. He asked me for the information and sent for the previous X-ray.

* * * *

About a week later I received a call from the local doctor's office asking me to come in. When I arrived, the doctor told me that the previous X-ray had arrived. We looked closely at it. There was no question about the bone spur. It was prominent in the earlier X-ray on the front of my right shoulder, obvious and protruding forward. No question; no doubt. There it was.

Next we examined the new X-ray again. Where was the bone spur? We couldn't find it—neither the doctor nor I. It wasn't there. It was gone. The bone spur was gone! It was on my shoulder before, but it is gone! A very, very slight bit of shading marked the area on the new X-ray, as if to show where it *had* been, but it was there no longer. So I did not need surgery. The shoulder has given me no problems in that area since, and no new bone spur has developed.

Lord God, in Jesus's name, You did a miracle—again! You spared me from needing surgery—again! You demonstrated Your reality in this world—again!

"Beloved, I pray that all may go well with you and that you may be in good health, as it goes well with your soul" (3 John 1:2 ESV).

4

MELANOMA: NEGLIGENCE OVERRULED!

═══════════════

When I was young, I used to hear various sayings over and over again from different adults. Usually a repeated saying was preceded by the words "they say." I never was able to find out who "they" were. Some of the sayings had some truth and value; others did not. Incidentally, my parents were rarely—almost never— guilty of repeating the sayings that were worthless. I could name some of the adults who were, but I won't. One saying that was widely spread was "What you don't' know can't hurt you." Over time, I have come to learn the falsity of that one.

One time during my adult years, I developed a skin condition on my right forearm. I noticed that a small area of skin had darkened. Then, some weeks later, I noticed that it had actually turned black. However, life was busy, and there were some major things going on; so I didn't dwell on the question of the black area on my forearm. I entered a new profession, we moved to a new city, and I actually stopped noticing the black area.

Then about eight months later, I thought about it again and went to see a doctor to have it looked at. The doctor was not a specialist, dermatologist, or skin doctor. He did not identify any serious problem and prescribed something to treat the skin surface.

I applied the medication every day as instructed, but nothing improved. So after several weeks, I went back to see the doctor. He looked at my arm and prescribed something else to apply to the skin. I returned to see him in another two to three weeks, in the month of March. When I returned and the doctor saw that there was no improvement, he decided to perform a biopsy for the labs to analyze. He carved out the entire black area, which by this time was an oval more than an inch long.

A couple of weeks passed, and I didn't hear anything from the doctor. Then it had been three weeks. Well, you know the saying: "No news is good news"—another of those fallacious sayings. I reasoned that if there had been a problem, they would have notified me. So essentially, the subject dropped off my radar screen. I temporarily forgot about the whole matter, and my busy life went on.

Now, this had been the month of April. Fast-forward to June, when I received a statement in the mail from a medical facility in another city. The statement was vague, nondescriptive. I had never been to that medical facility, so I put the statement aside. Besides, if it were legitimate, my insurance would take care of it.

I received another statement in the mail around the first of August, a nondescriptive duplicate of the prior statement. I decided to make a phone call to the facility. I explained that I had never been to their place and asked what this was about.

The lady at the other end of the line said that a tissue sample had been sent to them in March, and that the charges were for the lab diagnosis. I asked what the results had shown. She said she didn't know, but that she was confident that everything had been sent to the clinic in my city.

By this time it was midafternoon on a Friday. I picked up the phone again and called to speak to my doctor. I was able to reach his nurse. I asked her if they had received a report of the results from the biopsy, and if so, what it said. She said she didn't see any report, but would look further and get back to me.

A half-hour later, my phone rang, and I heard the anxious voice of my doctor on the other end. "Bill, you've got to get in here right away." "Right away," of course, meant Monday, as this was late on Friday afternoon. The doctor went on to tell me that he had just read the lab report that stated that the tissue sample was melanoma, a fast-moving cancer.

During the weekend I learned that melanoma is a cancer that originates in the pigment-producing cells of the skin. I also learned that it readily spreads to distant parts of the body, where it continues to grow and destroy tissue. I also learned that it may spread through the lymphatic and blood vessels and can cause death within months. Needless to say, my weekend was highly charged with suspense.

On Monday morning I met with the doctor. He carved out a larger area from my right forearm—an area that completely surrounded the previous tissue sample. I referred to this as a "chunk" of flesh. I still have the scar—about four inches long. His obvious concern—and mine—was that the cancer may have spread. He said he would monitor the lab closely and strongly insist that they get the results to him by the end of the week. That meant five more days of suspense, during which I was seriously considering and planning what I needed to do to prepare to die in a few months.

I went in on Friday and received good news—the doctor said that I had made his day. The tests indicated that the melanoma had not spread. I told him God had made my day—my week, too.

Abba, Father—You protected me again. You kept the melanoma from spreading, even through months and months of negligence on my part, negligence by the doctor, and negligence by the lab. You overruled it all! Thank you again, Father!

"We give praise *and* thanks to You, O God; we praise *and* give thanks; Your wondrous works declare that Your Name is near and they who invoke Your Name rehearse Your wonders." (Psalm 75:1 AB)

5

CHEST PRESSURE: GOD DEMONSTRATES HIS WATCHFUL CARE

_I_n the early autumn of 2005, I experienced some episodes of pressure in my chest, which I interpreted as possible feelings of hunger or indigestion. When I mentioned the experiences while at the Mayo Clinic, the cardiologist ran some tests, took some measures, and told me that if I were to experience that again, and if the feeling of pressure were to last more than twenty minutes, I should go to an emergency room. The doctor there should immediately contact cardiology at the Mayo Clinic.

I did not experience the chest pressure again for perhaps two months. Then one afternoon, as I was doing a light workout, the pressure came on. I sat down to wait, and got into a conversation with one of the other men there.

After a while, I realized that more than twenty minutes had passed while I continued to experience the symptoms, so I called my wife and told her where I was going, then went to the emergency room at the nearby hospital.

The staff there examined me and admitted me to the hospital, where I was monitored all night. At about five thirty in the morning, the doctor returned. More tests were run, and he cleared me to travel the 450 miles to the Mayo Clinic in Rochester, Minnesota, where they would be expecting me. I was instructed to be a passive rider in our van, with my wife driving. He also pointed out the medical centers along the way. (Actually, there would be long stretches between very small communities.)

Our travel went well, without any incident.

In about seven to eight hours, we arrived at the main entrance of the Mayo Clinic. Attendants met me there, put me into a wheelchair, and rolled me to the desk for unscheduled appointments, where I was admitted and was to wait. I had been waiting there, sitting quietly in the wheelchair only about five minutes, when I began to feel strong pressure in my chest. I signaled to staff, and attendants came and whisked me up to the cardiology department, where the specialists examined me and administered some steps.

The cardiologist told me he was sending me to St. Mary's Hospital, to intensive care. He said it was only ten blocks away but that they would take me there by ambulance, which they did. Two attendants came in, put me on a gurney, took me to the elevator and down to an ambulance. In minutes I was flat on my back in a hospital room where I spent the night with constant, regular monitoring and excellent care.

In the morning, I was wheeled to an operating room for an angiogram, in which doctors fed a tiny camera through an artery to view the interior of the artery and see what blockage there was. The anesthesia put me out, so I was unconscious for a few hours.

After I had regained consciousness and was again back in my room, the doctor came to see me. He told me that based on the tests and the nature of my past symptoms, they had fully expected that it would be necessary to conduct bypass surgery or to install a stent in an artery. However, he said that the results from the angiogram showed much less blockage in the artery—down to no more than 30 percent—and thus no surgery would be needed.

I was issued nitroglycerin and released to go home. I carried the nitro with me for two to three years but only used it twice—both times during the first six months, when I felt symptoms so mild that I wasn't really sure if they were the real thing.

- Lord God, Abba Father—You watched out for me again, and in such a way that I knew it was You. You protected me from having a chest-pressure episode throughout that 450-mile drive, during most of which there were no medical facilities nearby.

- Then You allowed the episode to happen just five minutes after I had arrived at the Mayo Clinic, where they could deal with it. Your timing was exact so I would know that it was Your hand that had protected me
- Then during the night, you significantly reduced the artery blockage that had caused the severe symptoms—so severe that the specialists had expected that they would need to do bypass surgery or install a stent.
- You are indeed the Great Physician!

"Casting the whole of your care—all your anxieties, all your worries, all your concerns, once and for all—on Him; for He cares for you affectionately, and cares about you watchfully" (1 Peter 5:7 AB).

6

FIRST THINGS FIRST

_____

We all have our priorities, and we usually think we have most things worked out to meet our priorities. But sometimes we need a little nudge or a gentle wake-up call.

I was in Grand Forks one pleasant summer day and decided to stop by to see Betty, an elderly retired lady who was living in an assisted-living apartment building there in the city. Betty had just recently moved to this place from a town about thirty miles away. One of her main reasons for moving here was to be near a younger sister. Betty herself was a mature Christian believer who prayed faithfully and regularly for many people, including her sisters.

While there, after some conversation, Betty asked me if I would take her to visit her sister, Linda, who was living in an apartment in another part of the city. I agreed.

As we were on our way, Betty explained that Linda had a physical condition that caused her chronic pain. Betty said she hoped that we could pray for Linda's health. I asked Betty if Linda was a Christian believer. She said she wasn't sure, but was concerned for her.

When we arrived, Betty introduced me to Linda. While Linda was up and about, I could see from her facial expressions and her movements that she was in considerable, constant pain.

After we had visited for a little while, I felt impressed to ask Linda's opinion about some spiritual things. For example, I asked her if she felt she was at the place in her spiritual experience where she could say that she knew she would go to heaven. She said she wasn't sure, but as the conversation went along, she indicated that she was open to discussing it. So we talked about what Jesus's death on the cross accomplished for her and how to "get in on it"—to receive His forgiveness and salvation. We talked about what it means to receive Him, as stated in John 1:12.

In a short while, Linda prayed and asked the Lord to forgive her, to come into her life, and to save her, which He did, as He promised in the Bible (1 John 5:9–15; Revelation 3:20; John 1:12). She was happy, Betty was happy, I was happy! Then I asked her if we could pray about her pain. Her response: "Oh, the pain is all gone!"

Lord, You did it again—first things first. Your first priority was salvation and Linda's direct relationship with You, and then right after that was taken care of,

You dealt with the pain! But then again, You did already tell us:

"But seek first the kingdom of God and His righteousness, and all these things will be added to you" (Matthew 6:33 ESV).

PART TWO

RESCUES

1

MOSCOW: RESCUED FROM AN AMBUSH

---

*H*ere I am, thinking about life in the abstract and thinking philosophically. But life doesn't take place that way. I recall a proverb that says, "Man plans his day, but life is what really happens." A few seconds—even one second—can change everything.

I had an opportunity to go to Russia with a mission organization to give out information about Jesus Christ to passersby on the downtown streets, principally in Moscow and St. Petersburg. I don't think it even entered my mind that there might be any risk of danger. However, I was soon to find out that such a risk was lurking just around the corner.

* * * *

I was amazed by the interest of the people in receiving the books and booklets we had brought. For example, one day in Moscow, our bus pulled into a large parking area in front of a sort of a mall and stopped. The staff got out and opened the luggage bins below, which were filled with our books and booklets. As the rest of us got off the bus, people began to gather around us—hundreds hurrying toward us from every direction. We began to hand out books as fast as we could, and more people kept coming, until the last person had a book and everyone had left.

On another occasion in the early afternoon I went into a downtown railroad station. I was alone. Of course, I was carrying my backpack filled with our books. I entered a waiting room where there were several dozen passengers sitting and waiting. As I entered, every eye turned to look at me. I remember thinking at the time, *It's as if they are all expecting me.* So I went along each row. Each person had his or her hand out for a book, and I had enough for everyone.

* * * *

Moscow has a huge subway system deep underground. I was told it was designed to serve also as an immense bomb shelter. Fast-moving escalators take you down or up. A huge ring encircles the city, while numerous other tracks cross the ring and extend further out as branch lines. Most of the areas down below ground are like museums.

What I remember most about Moscow are the people. One morning, a few of us were at a street entrance to the subway, giving books to people who were hurrying by. One man was rushing past me, and as I held out a book to him, he took it. He walked about twenty to thirty feet, stopped, opened the book, stepped back to the wall, and began to read. As I observed him, I said to myself, "But he *was* in a hurry to get someplace."

Another man took a book I offered him as he walked by quickly. He walked on about twenty to thirty feet, stopped, turned and smiled at me, then went on his way.

* * * *

On a Sunday afternoon, I went to an area on the edge of the business district in Moscow. There were not a lot of people on the street, but there were some. At one point I found myself in a conversation with a Moscow man who knew no English, but who was accompanied by his young daughter of maybe thirteen or fourteen, who could speak English quite well. So with her translating back and forth, we had a lengthy conversation, during which I explained the booklet (printed in Russian), presenting the four spiritual laws regarding how to know God, receive forgiveness, and have eternal life.

When we finished and they had left, I found myself alone on a deserted street. No cars. No people. Quiet. I had taken taxis several times in Moscow, however, and I was sure I could get a cab across the city to Gorky Park, where I would be meeting the other members of my group.

At this point, I was ushered into and out of one of those experiences you only read about. And when you read about them, there is never a happy ending. Such experiences are always unexpected, always unplanned—on one side.

When I was a kid of nine or ten, I listened to a radio program called *The Shadow.* Every night, the program was introduced by a sinister voice saying, "Who knows what evil lurks in the hearts of men?"

Soon a man came up to me and said that he was a cab driver and that he would take me to Gorky Park. He asked me if I would follow him to his cab, which was about two blocks away. "Sure," I said. All of my experiences that week had been positive, upbeat, good, happy, and uplifting. Did I have any reason to question? If I did, it wasn't occurring to me.

So we started to walk away from the business district. The next block became more like a warehouse district. The cab driver was walking fast and was now about fifty to a hundred feet ahead of me. I passed a man standing by a lamppost on the other side of the street who called out something to me in Russian that I didn't understand. We went on.

Suddenly I heard a loud voice about fifty to one hundred feet behind me calling out in English: "Excuse me! I have some questions. Do you have time to talk to me?" I whirled around. The spell was broken.

Yes, I have time to answer questions, I thought. *That's why I'm here.*

I think this man had spotted my backpack as he came around the corner behind me and had been hurrying to try to catch up with me. He said, "My name is Alex. I received one of your books yesterday, and I have questions. I've been looking for one of your people all day. I'll get you to where you need to go." I agreed and told Alex that I needed to get to Gorky Park, which was partway across the city.

"Oh, and by the way, Alex, did you notice that man by the lamppost back there?" Yes, he had noticed. "What was he shouting to me?"

"He was shouting a warning to you. 'He kill! He kill!'"

The man by the lamppost had been trying to warn me that I was being led into an ambush.

As I sit here, thinking about what happened, there is a lot to think about:

- Alex had received the book just the day before.
- He read it and, as a result, had many questions.
- He had searched Moscow all day in an attempt to find one of our group members. He found me. There. Just then. Right before I would have walked into a killer's ambush. If he had come around that corner just thirty seconds later, I would have been gone.
- Lord, Your timing was awesome. You rescued me. You spared my life—again.

"My times are in Your hands; deliver me from my enemies and from those who pursue me" (Psalm 31:15 NIV).

"I shall not die, but I shall live, and recount the deeds of the Lord." (Psalm 118:17 ESV).

2

LENINGRAD: TWILIGHT ZONE AT TWILIGHT

*D*ecisions. Decisions can lead into the unknown.

It was now another year, and I was back in Russia again, for an evangelism project. On one occasion after dinner, our team had the rest of the evening free. A few of us decided to leave the hotel and go to the nearby street market there in Leningrad, and we thought we knew what to expect. But I had no inkling, even in my most extreme imagination, of what I would face in just a little while.

This was my third time in Russia, and each time I found it more mysterious, more unpredictable, more potentially dangerous than any other part of Europe— or Asia—where I had spent some time. This evening would exceed even that.

We had been assigned a different hotel this time. It was not the huge one on the island where I had been before, where tourists were virtually sequestered away from the main city. Our present hotel was *in* the main city. Across the street from the hotel was a large open area at least two blocks long. There had once been buildings there, but the buildings had been bombed out during World War II, and nearly all of the rubble and debris had long since been cleared away. This is where the street market now was. There were dozens and dozens of tables of clothing, souvenirs, and everything else.

Now, in the early evening of dusky Leningrad, the crowds of people were thinning out. It was still daylight, but it was beginning to dim. As I walked around, I eventually found myself out at one edge of the market. Suddenly there were two men in front of me, in my face, challenging me to a fight. Why?

In Russian, there is a word, translated as "hooligan," that is used to describe someone who seeks to cause trouble and to pick fights for no reason other than that that's the way they are. These two guys were hooligans, and they wanted a fight. They were two pretty big, young guys in good physical shape, probably in their middle twenties, and I was more than twice their age and not nearly as agile, as strong, or as quick as I once was. Two to one—not good odds.

Not good odds at all. How do I get out of this? How do I get away from this?

Their fists in midair, ready to strike-- but suddenly it got quiet. Their bodies stopped moving, with their fists still in midair. Their bodies frozen like statues. Heads not moving. Eyes not moving. Not a blink. Not even a twitch. My instincts told me, "Don't step back," so I took a step to my left. I looked at them. Neither of the hooligans moved. Their bodies did not turn, nor did their heads. Their eyes did not shift. So I took another big step to my left. I looked at their faces again. Still no movement from either of them. They were both still facing and focused on where I had originally been standing—frozen like two statues.

I started to walk, briskly and straight ahead, all the way across the street market, away from them. Something prompted me, *Don't look back.* I thought of Lot's wife, who *did* look back. I did not look back.

* * * *

Lord, I don't know what that was all about, but I do know this: You were watching over me, and You protected me. Again. Lord, it looked to me as if You instantly paralyzed both of those men. Or did You move either them or me into a different 'time dimension'? I recently read in a devotional book that Jesus said, in essence, "I can bend time." That must have been what You did that day in Leningrad. Lord, You are awesome!

As was once wisely said, "For some of us, no explanation is needed. For others, no explanation is possible."

"Bend down and listen to me; rescue me quickly. Be for me a great rock of safety, a fortress where my enemies cannot reach me" (Psalm 31:2 NLT).

3

THE BIGGEST ANGEL AND CURIOSITY AT SEVENTH AND HENNEPIN

C uriosity. A quality common to teenagers—an understandable quality. It is interest in what at the moment might be unknown. Sometimes, it is better that it remains unknown.

Teenagers. I was a teenager. My friend Denny and I had some free time, it was a Friday night and we were just messin' around. We found ourselves down on Hennepin Avenue, in downtown Minneapolis. Not just Hennepin Avenue, but Seventh and Hennepin. As a couple of teenage guys, we had no business being down there that night; we were just curious. I don't know what we were looking for--or curious about--but there we were.

We were standing on the sidewalk, just outside one of the many bars in that area, when suddenly a great big guy came up behind Den and grabbed him by the back of his neck, startling Den. The guy half-growled in a snarling, threatening tone, "Hey, what are you guys doing here?"

I looked at this guy. He was *huge*. He looked to be as tall or taller than the biggest of professional football linemen, and he was just as heavy, muscular, and powerful. And he had Den by the back of his neck and we were both startled way beyond words.

But as fast as that had happened, there was suddenly an *even bigger* guy behind the first big guy. I don't know where he came from. This guy looked to be well over seven feet tall—maybe eight feet—and as I think back, he looked as big, powerful, and menacing as that gigantic green cartoon character who bursts his shirt when he transforms from being just a regular guy, except that this giant of a man had a totally clean-cut, all-American look to him, with a face like Superman or Tim Tebow. He was huge and powerful.

As quickly as he appeared, he grabbed the first big guy by the back of *his* neck and said loudly, "Leave these guys alone!" The first guy let go of Den, and we took off running. We kept running until we reached my car about a block away. We never looked back, but jumped into my car and drove away.

* * * *

What happened back there after we were gone? I haven't the slightest idea. But that second guy was an angel sent by God to rescue us. Humans don't get that big or move that fast. By the way, Den and I never talked about going back there again. So much for curiosity.

Wow, Lord, You are awesome! You are amazing. You really are watching over us. You rescued us. Again!

"He rescued me from my strong enemy ..." (Psalm 18:17 ESV).

"The angel of the Lord encamps around those who fear Him, and delivers them" (Psalm 34:7 ESV).

4

FIFTEEN FEET FROM DEATH

I was fortunate and blessed to have a praying mother. More than that, I was blessed to have a praying mother who prayed *for me*. She didn't talk about it much, but as I look back, I can see the effects. I see her prayers and her gentle influence. I remember many random incidents that turned out not to be so random after all, and little influences that stuck in my mind and made a difference.

Second Chronicles 16:9a says, "The eyes of the Lord range throughout the earth, seeking to show Himself strong on behalf of those whose hearts are loyal to Him."

As I write this, I recall an incident that could have changed and altered the course of my life or ended it right there. I was a student in college and was working part time as a busboy at the Minneapolis Athletic Club, mostly in its thirteenth-floor dining room. After finishing work for the day and turning in my heavily starched white uniform, I left the building and was walking south along Marquette Avenue to return to the college campus. It was a winter afternoon. As I crossed Seventh Street and was approaching the curb ahead of me, I suddenly heard a loud crash to my right, and a car, partially airborne, sailed toward and crashed into the lamppost only a little more than fifteen feet in front of me.

At the time, I was startled by the crashing noise and the suddenness and closeness of what had just happened. Just a few degrees difference and the flying car could have landed on me instead of smashing into the lamppost. Or if I had been only a few steps ahead, the car would have landed on me. Yet I was only a little rattled, and with my teenage mind, I thought of this incident more as a conversation topic—a close call I could tell my friends about. But I don't recall that I ever did talk about it, and life went on.

I have more recently come to realize that it was the hand of God that protected me. A few seconds could have altered or ended my life that winter afternoon, but they didn't, thanks to the mercy and watchful care of God and a praying mother.

Lord, You kept me safe—again! I thank You—again.

"The Lord protects him and keeps him alive; He is called blessed in the land ..." (Psalm 41:2a ESV).

5

WHITEOUT ON I-29

---

*F*ather, I thank You that life has a purpose—that *my* life has a purpose—and that I am surrendered to You so that my life can be part of Your purpose. I wasn't always surrendered to You, but You knew the time would come when I would be.

Sometimes life presents some huge risks, and usually we don't have any idea that we are on a collision course with a major, dangerous event that just takes over. Whatever plans we had are suddenly overturned. I think of a day in early March when I set out from northwest Minnesota on a thirteen-hundred-mile drive to Colorado to meet my wife, stay a few days there, and drive back together to Minnesota.

My planned route for the first day took me to I-29, south through Grand Forks and Fargo, North Dakota, and then on to Sioux Falls, South Dakota, where I had reserved a motel room for the night.

The first part of my journey was pleasant and without incident. The skies were mildly overcast, and there was a slight wind. Leftover snow on the ground served as a reminder that winter hadn't actually left yet. However, as I drove along, the possibility didn't even cross my mind that I might not reach Sioux Falls.

Eventually I arrived at Grand Forks, and as I approached the city, snow began to fall, lightly at first. Along with the snow came a slight but steady wind, which began to blow the snow across my path.

I passed through the edge of the city and continued south. Fargo was about seventy-five miles ahead—only a little more than an hour away-- or so I thought. The snow continued to fall. Moderate snow, pushed across the freeway in front of me by a steady wind, blowing from the west. No problems. I had been out and had driven through falling snow—even storms—many times.

Suddenly, everything went white. It was as if all of a sudden I had entered a cloud. I could not see the road at all. No signs. No fence posts. No landmarks. I could barely even see part of the hood of my car. I could hear the wind, and I could feel it pushing on the right side of the car, one powerful gust after another.

I slowed down to a crawl, maybe a walking pace. I knew I had been in the left lane, so I had to be careful not to drift off the edge. I felt it when I went off onto the gravel shoulder, and I opened my door to see where the edge was. I kept it open just a little—I had to.

Since the powerful wind and snow were blowing across from my right, I discovered that there was a little sheltered area low on my side of the car--so when I had my door open, I could look down there and see where the edge of the pavement was.

I had to stay by the edge. If I got away from this edge, I would have no way of knowing where I was
.What if another car or truck came up behind me? I couldn't think about that.

I was moving very slowly, but I had to keep moving. I had to keep moving. If I went off the pavement, I could just barely feel the crunch of the gravel. Keep moving.

Watch the edge of the road.

I totally lost track of the passing of time, but it must have been hours. *Keep moving. Keep watching the edge.*

During all this time I did *not* see even one car or truck.

Now the white was dimming to a light gray. But the wind continued to shove and shake the car. It continued getting a little darker. *What was that? A sign? A sign!* But by the time I could make it out, I was passing it. It was an exit sign for Fargo, but I couldn't see where the ramp was.

After a time, I caught a faint glimpse of another exit sign. Too late—and besides, there was no way to see where to drive. I couldn't see where the exit ramp was. Getting dark now. I couldn't even see where the road was. *Somewhere up ahead there's one more exit sign for Fargo. One last exit. After that—open country again. And it's dark. And impossible to see where the edge of the pavement is.*

One last exit somewhere up ahead.

Powerful, angry wind gusts shoving against the car. Blinding snow.

Getting darker.

Suddenly—*what was that?* I could barely see it. *A truck?* With the blowing snow I couldn't be sure. Yes, there was a large truck alongside me on my right, passing me very, very, gradually—an eighteen-wheeler flatbed truck--the first and only vehicle I had seen for hours. He very gradually pulled ahead of me, and just then I thought I caught a faint glimpse of the last exit sign for Fargo.

The truck turned off the road, and I saw that I had this last opportunity—this one and only opportunity—to get off the freeway; so I followed him off the freeway and up the ramp. He went on up the ramp and disappeared.

Now there were large, strong evergreen trees on both sides of me, which cut the wind, making it much easier to see as I drove around the curve. I spotted a nearby gas station. I pulled across and went into the small convenience store. The name of a good friend popped into my brain—a newspaper columnist for the *Fargo Forum.* So I called him. He and his wife invited me to come and stay the night at their home. Wonderful friends.

The storm was so severe, as it turned out, that the freeway was not opened until after ten o'clock the next morning. As I drove south that morning, I saw many, many cars, trucks, and vans off the road—some upside down, some on their sides. I started to count but stopped counting in a few minutes when I reached a hundred.

Lord, I couldn't see in that whiteout, but You could see me! And You sent that truck. That was Your angel and Your special truck. There had not been even one car or truck for several hours on that freeway, but You sent that one at the exact time when he could show me the way and lead me to the ramp to get off the freeway. You spared me in an amazing way! How can I adequately thank You for Your mercy, Your care, and Your watchfulness over this person? I am so grateful to You.

You spared me!
You rescued me!
Again!

"O give thanks to the Lord, call upon His name; make known His doings among the peoples!" (1 Chronicles 16:8 AB).

"For He will command His angels concerning you to guard you in all your ways" (Psalm 91:11 ESV).

PART THREE

IT'S GOD'S CAR, AND HE LETS ME DRIVE IT

1

FINDING THE CAR

---

*I*t can be surprising that what begins as a small task or project can become much more. A simple decision can turn into a whole series of steps, sometimes involving much more time than ever might have been imagined.

When I accepted a position with Northwestern College in St. Paul, I also began to search for a new car—a search that turned out to be by far the most thorough search I had ever been involved in. I read everything I could find on the subject of reliability, frequency of repairs, customer satisfaction, and gas mileage, and I decided that for that year and for recent years, the Buick LeSabre was the car to buy.

Since I had for years passively dreamed of owning a deep red car, I put that on my list. And since I would likely be in this car for many hours, I decided that it would be very nice if the interior matched the outside. I decided on leather upholstery for ease in sliding in and out, and a V6 would be just fine.--and a four-door model with a bench front seat.

Armed with this list of criteria, I began the search. As a result of contacting and visiting several dealers and car lots, I learned that my combination of interior and exterior colors, combined with leather upholstery, was impossible to find in the Minneapolis-St. Paul area. So I contacted a local credit union to conduct a four-state search. They came back with nothing. I contacted another agency to conduct a five-state search. They also came back with nothing.

By now, time was running out for me. I had prayed about this many times. Why should this be so difficult? Was I asking too much? I was down to my last day. I had learned of a car in St. Cloud with my color on the exterior and with leather seats, but it had a tan interior. I was about to go to St. Cloud (about fifty miles away), but just before I left, my attention was brought to the existence of a car at a dealership in Hastings, about thirty miles south of St. Paul. I called, went out there, and found it to be *exactly* what I had been searching for. And on the last day!

Because of the way things worked out, I began to say that this is "God's car, and He lets me drive it."

Lord, thank You that I found this car—and on the last day, at the last hour! How could this be a big thing? Actually, looking back, it shouldn't have been a big thing at all. And yet You showed me that even in the small things, You care about us. I thank You, and I thank You many times over.

Everybody in our family has heard me say this is "God's car, and He lets me drive it!" Incidentally, I have driven a lot of miles ... but that's another story.

"For this God is our God for ever and ever; He will be our guide even to the end" (Psalm 48:14 NIV).

2

HE LIFTS ME OUT OF TROUBLE IN SIOUX FALLS

―――――――――

Winters in South Dakota are unpredictable. In fact one of the most predictable things about South Dakota winters is that it will be impossible to predict the next thing that will be unpredictable.

It was our first year back in the Midwest from the warm country. We had been away from really cold winters long enough to have almost forgotten what winter can be like in the upper Midwest.

Winter had arrived suddenly in South Dakota. Of course, it was about time—maybe even overdue. After all, it was November, and summer had seemingly extended and stretched way beyond what was typical. So, when winter swept across the plains from the north and west, there was nothing that was able to stop it or even slow it down.

One day, the sun had been shining through blue skies. What breezes there were, were gentle and pleasant. The temperature was just right; you didn't' even need to wear a sweater.

Then overnight, everything changed. Everything.

Sometime during the night, the gentle breezes were pushed aside and replaced by high-powered, howling winds. The pleasant temperature was gone, replaced by frigid air, and it seemed that the mercury had dropped down so rapidly and so far that it had fallen out of the bottom of the thermometer.

The green grass was gone—covered (as was everything else) with ever-increasing waves of drifting snow, which whistled around the corners of the buildings and sailed at high speed across every open space, stacking up ever higher and deeper, ever higher and deeper. This was now a totally different world from the day before.

Eventually, the vicious fury of the wind and snow had run its course. Everything became still and quiet. The wind was gone, but the snow was here. Much snow.

Here and there a door would open. People would appear, carrying a shovel or walking behind a snow blower. Then the rumble of "heavy artillery" could be heard in the distance as big trucks with snowplows swung into action and began pushing the snow to the sides of the streets.

This was the scene in Sioux Falls, South Dakota, when I arrived on the following day. Most of the streets had been plowed, and some of the snow had been hauled away.

I took this all in as I drove along a street, heading to an appointment. I was driving through an area of new construction. Some of the houses were completed. Others were only partially built. The progress of the construction crews had been interrupted by the powerful snowstorm that had suddenly ushered in the invasion of winter.

I pulled up to a corner and turned to the right. As I did, the right front corner of my car dropped what seemed to be most of a foot straight down. I just sat there. This was a new part of the city, and the streets weren't totally finished yet, but traffic was normal. I had turned where the street appeared to go, but I had misjudged. It appeared that everything was level. But I had been deceived. Deceived by a snow bank. Deceived by what was left of a snow bank, scraped off smooth and level.

What was I to do now? My right front drive wheel was down, floating in midair. I thought about my situation, but I didn't have to think about it for very long—only a few seconds at most. Now in my situation, even a few seconds could seem like an eternity, but nevertheless, a few seconds was all it was before the right front corner of my car raised straight up again. The car moved ahead, and I was clear from the problem and able to be on my way!

"He drew me up from the pit of destruction, out of the miry bog, and set my feet upon a rock, making my steps secure" (Psalm 40:2 ESV).

If I substitute *snow bank* for *miry bog*, and *wheel* for *feet* ... Lord, I recognize that this verse from Psalms is metaphorical, but what You did was literal—then, this is what is being said:

"He drew me up from the snow bank, and set my wheel upon the street, making my path secure" (Psalm 40:2, paraphrased).

3

FARGO: A LIFT AND A PUSH

One of the worst things about danger is that it may creep up on you while you are totally unaware of it. You may not even suspect the presence of danger until you are totally surrounded and it is ready to pounce.

I thought about this one winter night when my wife, Yvonne, and I were traveling several hundred miles on our way home. It was a long drive, and shortly after it had become dark, I began to reminisce about other winter adventures. I thought of a time just a few years before—an experience in a Fargo, North Dakota winter.

* * * *

There had been several days of mild weather in which the snow on the ground had almost been melting in the bright, clear sunshine. Today was like that. I got into the car to drive from the far southwest of Fargo, eastward across the city, and into the neighboring city of Moorhead, Minnesota. It almost seemed as if winter was coming to an end, although I knew that that was far from being true. I hadn't checked any weather reports. I had no reason to think there would be any problems.

I wasn't thinking about it at the time, but as I drove through Fargo, there were few trees. As I crossed the state line into Moorhead, though, there were almost suddenly a lot of trees. The contrast was striking. This fact would become significant later.

I arrived in Moorhead and went inside the building to attend to business, which ended up taking about two hours. During that time, I gave no thought about weather outside.

When I left to return to my car, it had become dark outside, although it was only late afternoon. However I did not consider that particularly unusual, since during the winters in Fargo, it did typically get dark in the latter part of the afternoon. I also noticed that the temperature had dropped and that three to four inches of snow had already fallen. The car was surrounded with snow packed against the wheels. There was a wind, but it wasn't blowing hard. Of course--the trees. But I didn't think about that at the time.

I managed to get the car away from the curb and headed for home. The streets seemed unusually quiet, especially for this time of day.

I drove across Moorhead and crossed into Fargo. As I drove, the wind became stronger and stronger. The snow was now coming down faster and faster. As I reached the western part of Fargo, there were large areas where there were no houses and no buildings of any kind. And of course, no trees. The wind was growing even more powerful. The snow was now coming down ever faster and ever more forcefully.

I began to notice that the snow was accumulating on the streets. When was the last time I had seen a car or any kind of a vehicle? There should be a lot of traffic at this time. But there was none—absolutely no one. I was the only one out there.

The snow on the street was getting deeper and deeper as I drove toward home. Now I could hear it beginning to rub on the bottom of the car. Were the snowplows not out? Had the city and county pulled the plows? I had heard of that happening during particularly severe storms before. But this time, I was out in the storm. And the snow was getting so deep that it was rubbing on the bottom of my car. Could I get home?

I kept driving, pushing and forcing my way through the snow.

Finally, there it was—our building and the entrance to the parking lot! I had to drive up a short incline to get up into the parking lot from the street. I made it partway up so that the front of the car was up but the back was still down in the street. The ramp was slippery and covered with several inches of snow. I tried several times but could not move up into the parking lot. The gale force wind outside the car was howling. I was not dressed for this. The snow was now coming down with blinding force. I sat there.

Suddenly, it was as if some powerful person or

persons took hold of my rear bumper, lifted the rear of the car, and pushed it up into the parking lot. I looked around but could see no one there. I was able to drive to the garage, drive the car inside, get out, stagger across the parking lot against the powerful wind to the apartment building, and get inside. I collapsed into a chair, gasping for air for several minutes while my wife attended to me.

By morning, the wind had died down, and more than two feet—and possibly up to three feet—of new snow had accumulated through the night. It took several days before the streets had been cleared. During the first couple of days, the crews were only able to clear one side of each street, so motorists had to adjust

By the way, as if to accentuate the seriousness of the storm and the heavy snowfall, a member of a family that we were acquainted with in our apartment building suffered a heart attack during the early morning—at about daybreak. The ambulance was unable to get to him until the services of a large snowplow and driver were engaged. The plow literally cleared a path along the streets from the hospital to our parking lot, with the ambulance following right behind. As result, our friend survived.

* * * *

Abba Father, You did it again. You got me home. You gave my car a lift and a push, and You took care of everything. I thank You. Oh, I thank You again!

"He is a Savior and Deliverer, and He works signs and wonders in the heavens and on the earth ..." (Daniel 6:27a AB).

"I will ponder all Your work, and meditate on Your mighty deeds" (Psalm 77:12 ESV).

4

WHAT COULD HAVE HAPPENED ...

S ometimes, the best thing that can happen is that
something *doesn't* happen.

It was a dark and cold January night—about zero
degrees Fahrenheit—and I needed to drive from Fargo,
North Dakota to Sioux Falls, South Dakota, where I had
several appointments on the following days. That was
about a 250-mile drive in the middle of a cold, winter
Sunday night.

I arrived at the motel in Sioux Falls at about one
o'clock in the morning, checked in, went up to my room,
lay down, and slept soundly until my alarm awakened
me at seven. Nothing unusual so far. I performed my
usual morning routine, including prayer, preparation,
breakfast, and checking my laptop computer, and then

I went out to the car, warmed it up, and headed to my first appointment. Still nothing unusual so far.

I had driven no more than fifteen or twenty blocks when suddenly some fluid came shooting up from under the hood onto the windshield, spraying all over it so I couldn't see where I was going. There were no cars parked along the curb, so I was able to move to the right. Right there, there was an entry to a parking lot with a bank at one end and a funeral home at the other end. I pulled into the near end, stopped, and shut off my engine. I released the hood latch and got out. I looked back, and what I saw was a trail of leaked fluid from the street to the back of my car and a large pool of the same fluid under the car and expanding out from there on the pavement.

I called the local auto dealer. They came and got the car and took me to the dealership and then to my motel. A fluid line had burst, and they would have the car ready by the next morning. I spent the day taking care of business, including writing reports.

First thing the next morning, the driver brought my car to the motel, and I was back in business. But I had had plenty of time to think about what could have happened, what might have happened, and what did happen.

I had just driven for several hours in the middle of the night, on a Sunday night—a cold winter night. The route from Fargo to Sioux Falls runs almost entirely through desolate, open country. The line could have burst out there, but it didn't. Instead, I was able to get all the way to Sioux Falls and get a good night of restful sleep.

The next morning, I had been driving on busy streets and crossing through intersections with heavy traffic. I don't even want to think what might have happened if the line had burst in any of those situations, spraying my windshield as it did so I could not see. The line could have burst there, but it didn't.

Lord, my God, You held it together until I was away from heavy traffic and had turned onto a street where there were—amazingly—no cars in front or behind me or in the approaching lane.

You allowed me to reach the middle of the block, exactly to the place where I could turn in to that parking lot. There You allowed the line to burst. You watched out for me so that I remained safe, and was only barely inconvenienced at all!

"For the Lord loves the just and will not forsake His faithful ones. They will be protected forever ..." (Psalm 37:28a NIV).

5

Transmission Failure: A Minimum of Inconvenience

*S*ometimes what matters most isn't what *happens*. Sometimes what matters most is *when* it happens, and sometimes it is *where* you are when it happens.

It was a winter day—a day that started out pretty much like any other day. There was nothing notable, nothing out of the ordinary. I had an important meeting to attend in the morning. I also had business to take care of, mostly in town but some of it out in the country. There were people to see, which meant country driving out to a farm and later more driving to another farm.

The day went smoothly—no problems, no surprises. So far, so good. Now, it was about four o'clock in the afternoon. I pulled into the large parking lot of one of the local stores, and went inside to pick up a couple of items. I had pulled up into one of the marked lanes near the center of the parking lot.

When I came out of the store and walked to my car, I noticed that another car had *happened* to park in the marked spot directly in front of me. There was nothing unusual about that. It only meant that I would need to back out of my parking spot. That was no problem; I expect I would have backed out anyway.

I got into my car, started the engine, and shifted the automatic transmission into reverse. I stepped on the accelerator pedal lightly—just a little bit, as usual. Nothing *happened*. I tried it again. Foot on the brake, I shifted back to neutral and then to reverse again. Again nothing. Several repetitions—into park, back to reverse, into neutral, back to reverse. Nothing.

By this time, the driver had come, entered the car in front of me, and driven away. Now I could try driving forward, but that didn't work either.--But what if it had? I might not have known that my reverse gear would no longer function. I could have driven home without a reverse gear. But even if I could have pulled into my driveway, I wouldn't have been able to get out again without a working reverse gear. I checked my transmission fluid, and it was fine.

I was in this parking lot, which *happened* to be just two blocks from the garage where we regularly had our oil changed and regular repairs done. It was still early enough that they were still open, so I called. It so *happened* that the owner was there, so I talked with him.

He came and towed my car, and it so *happened* that

he had a transmission in his shop that was exactly like mine. He told me that he could complete the repair and charge me only a fraction of what it would normally cost through a dealer. I was able to get a ride home to where we lived, about fifteen miles out in the country, and my car was ready in two days.

Lord, you watched out for me again. I think of all the places and times the transmission *might have* failed:

- In my own driveway that morning, making me miss my meeting and appointments
- In someone's yard out in the country—resulting in much time lost and much inconvenience and expense
- At night

Instead, it *happened* just before the end of the day, with nothing pressing in my schedule. Also, the nearby garage *happened* to have an identical transmission on hand (for my nine-year-old car), saving much delay and saving me more than a thousand dollars.

"Why, you do not even know what will happen tomorrow. What is your life?" (James 4:14a NIV)

"You are the God who works wonders; You have made known Your might among the peoples" (Psalm 77:14 ESV).

6

FIVE HUNDRED MILES
OF ADVENTURE

───────────

*A*dventure is sometimes defined as a time when your life might be in danger. Yet sometimes the actual adventure can arise when something *doesn't* happen.

By this time, I had owned and driven the Buick— "God's car, and He lets me drive it"—for many years, and the odometer showed that it had run close to a quarter of a million miles. We had been living in the northwest part of Minnesota for several years, and we were now moving to the opposite side of the state.

The final day of packing and loading—a January day—turned out to be one of the coldest days of the winter. The shivering thermometer showed the temperature to be in the neighborhood of twenty-five degrees below zero

Fahrenheit—and getting colder. By late afternoon, the moving truck was loaded and gone. I took one last look around, locked the doors, got into the Buick, and drove out of the driveway for the last time. We had had many years of happy experiences with many good friends. Now it was time to turn the page and begin the next chapter of our lives.

I had remarked more than once that we often pray for ourselves or someone else to have safe travel. I would often add a word, asking for safe, *uneventful* travel, but then after the travel, we wouldn't know what unanticipated event or happening the Lord had spared us from.

I was about to embark on a journey of more than five hundred miles, driving in the dark during the coldest nights of the winter in a car with nearly a quarter of a million miles on the odometer. But this was God's car, and nothing bad had *ever* happened to me while driving this car. Furthermore, whenever any part of the car itself had worn out or quit, it had always happened at a time or location where I had only been barely inconvenienced, at most.

I turned the wheel and headed east into the gathering darkness. My destination that night was the city of Duluth. I would travel almost 250 miles. This was a Friday night. One of my daughters and two of my grandchildren were already in Duluth for an ice skating competition. My granddaughter would be skating the next day, and I was looking forward to watching as she skated in the events.

My travel to Duluth was uneventful and without problems. But then, I didn't expect any problems. The skating went well, my granddaughter won some awards, and we all enjoyed the day. By the time everything was finished, it was late afternoon, and by the time we had eaten dinner, it was dark outside.

We started south in our two vehicles. Our first destination would be Minneapolis, and then we would head further south—a total of about 275 to 300 miles. Our routes would eventually diverge. After a time, we became separated on the highway, but we encountered no problems on this cold, winter Saturday night.

I reached Minneapolis, and then continued south. Eventually, at about midnight, I arrived at our new home. I drove into the garage, closed the big door, and went into the house—a nice, warm, secure home.

* * * *

I didn't go out into the garage on Sunday, so it must have been Monday morning when I opened the door and looked out into the garage. What greeted my eyes was a large pool of purple fluid, under and around the car, covering nearly a third of the floor of the garage.

I checked with two neighbors for recommendations, called the auto repair shop they suggested, and asked for a mechanic to come to tow the car to their shop.

When the car was up on the rack, the mechanic told me that the metal transmission line had burst and that they would need to send for a replacement. It would take a couple of days to get it. I told him I had just driven more than five hundred miles, and it had held together until I had arrived at home and parked in my own garage. God had provided and protected again!

The mechanic's response was, "Well, if it had been me, it would have burst way out in the country, in the middle of the night."

God, You did it again!

You held that metal line together through more than five hundred miles on those weekend nights, through two of the coldest nights of the winter, while I was traveling through long stretches of country.

And that was the adventure—experienced unawares. You watched over me. Again!

"Everything has been created through Him and for Him. He existed before everything else began and He holds all creation together" (Colossians 1:16b–17 NLT).

PART FOUR

I LEARN ABOUT PRAYER AND GOD'S HEART

1

WILL GOD ANSWER MY PRAYER?

═══════════════════

I remember reading that so many of us pray prayers that are so general, so vague, that when it comes down to the bottom line, we really have no way of knowing if God answered the specific prayer or not.

I had no doubt that God answered prayer in general. I had seen evidence over and over that He answered the prayers of others. I had indeed been protected due to the prayers of others for me. However, when it came down to the specific question of whether God would answer *my* prayer for someone to be healed, I had a lack of confidence. I prayed, and somewhere in the back of my mind, I had the confidence that my prayers made a difference. But I didn't believe that they made a difference in a way that I could point to as tangible or specific.

That was about to change.

One weekend, our church hosted a seminar on the subject of prayer and healing. I was very interested, so I attended. The seminar included instruction, demonstration, and training. During the course of the weekend, I had the opportunity to observe people actually being healed of a variety of physical problems on the spot.

The visiting team explained that in their church, as a regular practice, several teams of three or four would come to the front at the close of their services to pray with those who requested prayer for any reason. The praying was not done publicly but rather in small groups, each group meeting and praying informally at the same time.

Also, it is important to point out that in the training, we were instructed that if the person who has come for prayer is in pain, it is important that we pray specifically for the Lord to take away the pain. Then after praying, it is important to ask the person how he or she feels.

The leadership of our church thought this was a good idea, so we decided to put the plan into practice in our church as well. We formed several teams with three or four on each team, and I volunteered to be a member of one of the teams. I was comfortable with the arrangement, as I was just one of a group.

The composition of each team was fixed, and if someone were to be absent on a specific Sunday, the other three would be there. I was okay with it, as we entered into the praying together each week. None of us was singled out at any time, and I was there each week to pray along with my team.

This arrangement worked for me until one Sunday morning, when I made my way to the front at the close of the service and began looking for the other members of my team. The other teams were there and ready, but no one else from my team was there!

I tried to join another team, but the assistant pastor would not let me. He said our team was needed, as there were several people to be prayed with. But I was the only member of our team. It took a bit for the realities to sink in.

- Our team is needed to pray with someone.
- I am the only one here representing our team.
- I alone will be praying for and with someone.
- Results will be tangible, and known on the spot.

I took a deep breath.

The assistant pastor introduced me to a husband and wife. They explained to me that the wife had a serious condition internally and was in pain as we were standing there talking. The two of them had come for prayer, for the Lord to heal her. Crunch time. It was time to step up and put my faith on the line—time for real, serious business.

We went to prayer, the three of us standing there, facing each other in a small circle. This was a time for direct, specific praying, not a time for vagueness or generalities. I asked the Lord to heal the wife. I knew she was in pain. I asked the Lord to take away the pain.

When I had finished praying, I asked her how she

was feeling. She replied, "The pain is gone!" Both she and her husband were happy and excited. Needless to say, I was happy and excited too!

* * * *

Father God, You taught me some important lessons that morning, and You saw to it that I would indeed learn them. None of my other team members were there that morning. (I don't know of any other instance when that happened with any of the teams.) –but You didn't let me just blend in with another team.

You saw to it that I met someone with a tangible physical condition calling for a direct prayer—calling for a tangible answer—so we could all know when You answered.

You arranged, for my instruction, for me to be the one "on the spot," appointed to pray—and to pray directly and specifically.

And finally, Lord, You heard and answered the prayer—*my* prayer! You boosted my faith several notches that morning. I would never again be the same. Lord, You are wonderful!

Lessons:

Faith is confidence in God. Act on it.

I need never be hesitant in prayer again.

"And this is the confidence that we have toward Him, that if we ask anything according to His will, He hears us. And if we know that He hears us in whatever we ask, we know that we have the requests that we have asked of Him" (1 John 5:14–15 ESV)

"I will instruct you and teach you in the way you should go. I will counsel you with my eye upon you" (Psalm 32:8 ESV).

2

RAINDROPS STOP FALLIN' ...

---

*J*esus said that children were very important to Him. When His disciples tried to discourage some children from coming to Him, Jesus rebuked the disciples. He went on to tell them that, in fact, children were a priority with Him. What Jesus had to say about children is recorded in all of the first three gospels. Jesus went on to say that it is vital to receive and welcome the kingdom of God as a little child does. He said that the kingdom belongs to those who do.

We can learn from observing our little children. I have seen certain qualities in my own children and grandchildren, as they start out in life at their young, tender ages. The first charactcristic that comes to mind is that they are trusting—in parents, grandparents, and in God Himself.

I think of a day when this was really brought home to me:

We were living in northern Minnesota at the time, out in the country, in a beautiful area surrounded by tall pines and balsams. On this particular day, I was sitting and reading at our kitchen table, which was just inside two large glass doors that led out onto a deck in the back. It was late morning, and it was raining—one of those steady, late-summer rains that you could expect to continue all day.

As I continued to read, my little granddaughter, Jillian, came into the room and climbed up onto the chair next to me. Then she spoke.

"Papa," she said. "Will you ask God to stop the rain so I can go outside and play on the swing?" I stopped reading. How could I possibly deny my little granddaughter's expectant prayer request? She was a little child and certainly had the faith and trust of a little child. But what if I prayed and God did not stop the rain? Would the disappointment damage her faith?

She asked me again. "Papa, will you ask God to stop the rain so I can go outside and play on the swing?" I hadn't answered her, but I answered her now. I said yes, I would. I looked outside one more time at the relentless, steady rain coming down. Then I turned toward my granddaughter and began to pray—aloud. It was not a long prayer. I was carrying her request—and my request—to the Father, in Jesus's name. I *knew* He could stop the rain. Then I stood up and went across the room to the refrigerator to get a glass of something to drink.

It wasn't more than about two minutes before I heard Jillian's excited voice behind me. "Papa! Look. The rain stopped! God is listening to us!" She had been looking through the glass door, watching expectantly. I went to the door and looked outside. Yes, the rain had stopped!

I learned something that day—actually several things.:

My faith went up at least another notch or two.

- I learned that God cares about what matters to His little ones.
- He will honor the faith and trust of one of His little ones.
- Nothing is too small a matter for Him. (I had *already* learned that nothing is *too big* for Him to handle.)

His tender care was demonstrated again that day.

My little granddaughter's faith and trust in God were strengthened and confirmed.

Lord, You are so good!

"And He called a little child to Himself and put him in the midst of them, and said, 'Truly I say to you, unless you repent [change, turn about] and become like little children [trusting, lowly, loving, forgiving], you can never enter the kingdom of heaven at all. Whoever will humble himself therefore and become like this little child [trusting, lowly, loving, forgiving] is greatest in the kingdom of heaven'" (Matthew 18:2–4 AB).

3

GOD'S PATIENCE

Wisdom is wrapped up in learning lessons in life. Sometimes we learn a lesson that we weren't expecting to learn, and sometimes a lesson comes at a time when we were not anticipating it.

One day I received a phone call from a friend, Ray, asking me if I would go with him to visit his brother-in-law, whom I had never met. I said I would, so he came by and picked me up. It turned out that his brother-in-law, Al, lived out in the country on a farm. Al was retired and lived alone, as he had never married.

When we arrived, Ray introduced us. Al invited us in, and we went and sat in his kitchen, drinking coffee and talking about many things.

After a little while, our conversation came around to spiritual things. It turned out that Al knew very little about the subject, so I explained all about God's offer of salvation and eternal life through His Son, Jesus Christ. Ultimately, I asked him if he would like to pray and ask the Lord to save him. He said that he wasn't ready but that he would think about it, so we left it at that and went on to talk about something else.

When you witness, people don't forget what you said.

About a week later, Ray called me again. He said he was going out to see Al again and asked if I would like to ride along. I agreed, so we went.

In Al's kitchen again, at some point during the conversation, I asked him if he had had opportunity to think about our talk from the previous time. He said he had thought about it but still wasn't ready. I said okay and we went on to other topics.

* * * *

Almost a year later, I crossed paths with Al in a restaurant in town. Since I had last seen him, he had been in a devastating auto wreck, and he told me all about it. His car had been seriously crushed, and it required the jaws of life to pull it apart so he could be rescued from inside his car. He did have some permanent injuries, but was able to get around all right. His exact comment was, "I don't know why I survived."

My only response was, "I think God gave you more time." That's all I said.

* * * *

During the next couple of years, I crossed paths with him a few times, but I never brought up spiritual subjects.

Then one day, I heard that he had moved into the nursing home for the winter. Because of his physical condition, he didn't feel that it would be safe to stay out at his farm during the winter. I went to see him. He seemed comfortable and seemed to be doing all right. We talked about how he was doing and this and that. I did not bring up anything of a spiritual nature.

After a little while, I prepared to leave. I stood up, picked up my coat, and began to put it on. As I did, Al, in a very thoughtful tone of voice said, "Y' know..."--and paused.

I paused and looked at him. Often when someone begins with "Y' know ..." that person is about to say something that he or she has been giving a great deal of thought to.

Al spoke again. "Y' know, I remember about three years ago when you talked with me about surrendering to God. I wish I had." Then he paused and said again, "I wish I had."

I paused; I don't think I had used the phrase, "surrender to God," but he had gotten the point. He had understood what the issue was. He knew what was at stake. I said, "Al, is that something that you would still like to do?"

"Yes."

"Is that something that you would like to do *today*?"

"Yes."

I laid my coat down and sat down again. Then I went into a thorough explanation of the gospel with him. I explained God's love and mercy, our falling way short, and our need of a Savior. I spoke of God's Son, Jesus Christ, His death and resurrection, and what He accomplished for us. Jesus paid our fine and penalty, but to personally "get in on it," it was necessary for us individually to turn to Him, confess our shortcomings and need personally, and receive Him as Savior and Lord. I asked Al if this was the desire of his heart. He said yes. So we prayed. He prayed, confessed, and asked the Lord to save him and to come into his heart.

Then I said, "There is something I would like for you to do. There are two people who have been praying for you for a long time—your sister and your brother-in-law. I would like for you to tell them what took place here this afternoon." He said he would.

A few days later, I crossed paths with Ray, the brother-in-law. He said to me, "That sure was wonderful about Al."

"Oh, have you seen Al?"

"Yes, I have."

"What did he say?"

Ray gave me an accurate summary of what had taken place on that memorable afternoon the week before. Al had followed through.

God, You are so good, so merciful, and so patient. Indeed, You did give him time. You knew he would turn to You, and You didn't let him forget—even in three years!

"The Lord does not delay and is not tardy or slow about what He promises, according to some people's conception of slowness, but He is long-suffering [extraordinarily patient] toward you, not desiring that any should perish, but that all should turn to repentance" (2 Peter 3:9 AB).

"Good and upright is the Lord; therefore He instructs sinners in His ways" (Psalm 25:8 NIV).

4

PRAYERS ANSWERED: ONE LAST CHANCE

I recently heard someone say,
"When we pray, 'coincidences' happen.
When we don't pray, 'coincidences' don't happen."

Early one afternoon, I received a phone call from a lady asking me if I would go and visit her husband, Tom, in the hospital. He was there because he had suffered a heart attack. I agreed, and we arranged for a time a little later that same afternoon.

While driving to the hospital, I reviewed what I knew about Tom: he was an elderly man, perhaps in his seventies or eighties. I had attempted to visit with him once or twice in the past, but he seemed to have a serious hearing impairment, to the degree that he had seemed almost totally unable to hear or understand anything I said.

Also, by reputation, he was totally uninterested in anything related to God, the Bible, Jesus, or the church. If he had ever attended a church, it would have been many years in the past. On the other hand, Tom's wife, Barbara, was by contrast a definite believer and very actively involved in her church.

As I entered Tom's hospital room, I saw that Barbara was also there. Tom was in bed, sitting up. They both greeted me. We visited for a little while, but it was difficult because he would ask his wife to repeat everything I said. He seemed to better understand it when she said it. Perhaps it had a lot to do with lip reading, and if so, he was thus much more able to decipher what she said than what I said.

He tired soon, so I excused myself. But not before I asked if I might return the next day. Everyone agreed.

The next day, Barbara called and told me that Tom had not had a good night. She said Tom was weaker today and that his thinking was not nearly as clear. She suggested that we try again the following day, so we planned for that.

That day, and again on my way to the hospital the day after, I prayed asking the Lord to restore Tom's mind and to give him improved hearing so I could present the gospel to him. I asked the Lord to speak through me and to give him this one last chance.

When I walked into Tom's room, I could immediately sense that he was more alert, even much more so than he had been when I had visited him two days earlier.

He would respond to what I said and would only rarely ask Barbara to repeat anything. After a short while, I began to talk with him about spiritual matters. I asked him a question.

"Tom, if you were at heaven's gate, and the angel said to you, 'Why should I let you in?' what would your answer be?"

Tom, in a very indignant tone of voice, said, "Well! I'm as good as anybody else!"

I looked at him and said, "Tom, you may be as good as anybody else—and you may be better than most—but *none* of us is good enough." Then I asked him if he would be interested in seeing what the Bible says would be the right answer to the angel's question. Tom said yes, he would.

I had brought along some large print scripture verses, and I showed him Romans 3:23, "For all have sinned and come short of the glory of God" (KJV). It appeared that Tom got the point. I then showed him Romans 6:23, "For the wages of sin is death, but the gift of God is eternal life through Jesus Christ our Lord" (KJV).I explained the verse to Tom. He seemed to grasp it readily and without needing to ask his wife for any help. After seeing more scriptures about salvation, Tom was ready to pray.

* * * *

Following that visit, Tom remained in the hospital for a few days and then was placed in a nursing home for further care. I visited him there, and each time I prayed with him and brought him a page with scripture and teaching for Barbara to read to him later in the day. Barbara told me he looked forward to my visits. After a few days, the Lord took him home.

Lord, You are so merciful.

- You gave Tom that last chance.
- You gave him better hearing that day.
- You gave him better alertness.

I thank You, as I know Tom thanks You and Barbara thanks You.

"For He says, 'In the time of My favor I heard you, and in the day of salvation, I helped you.' I tell you, now is the time of God's favor, now is the day of salvation" (2 Corinthians 6:2 NIV).

PART FIVE

PROTECTION, SHIELD, AND PROVISION

1

NOT ENOUGH TIME TO PRAY

I'm sitting here in my living room, just thinking. Thinking about the fact that so many events in life can happen in an instant. You may be driving a car, and danger strikes. You can fall from a ladder—something that killed one of my uncles—with no time to see it begin to happen. There may be an explosion, like the one that killed my great uncle. There may be a sudden gunshot, a sudden heart attack or stroke, or a slip on the ice resulting in broken bones.

We all take precautions, and we also take out insurance--but the insurance policy does not prevent something from happening. Sometimes you can see something begin to happen, and yet there is nothing you can do to stop it from happening.

I had an experience like that one afternoon while driving from Coon Rapids to Anoka, a distance of about five miles. At the time, the highway there was three lanes wide. There was one lane northbound, one lane southbound, and one lane mainly used as a passing lane in both directions.

That particular spring afternoon, the sky was heavily overcast, and there was a light rain falling. The pavement was wet and a little slippery. There was a fair amount of steady traffic traveling in each direction.

Suddenly, I noticed one of the approaching cars begin to move from its right lane into the center lane. This would not have been especially notable, except that it was aimed straight at me. I first noticed it when it was a little more than a hundred yards away, but it was closing the distance rapidly. It was a black Ford, about a fifteen-year-old car. In a moment it had moved fully into the middle lane. Then it was a little bit into my lane, pointed directly at me. There was no way I could maneuver, because I was surrounded by traffic. Then it was a couple of feet into my lane and closing fast. Then it was right in front of me.

Suddenly, the car changed its direction, and veered across to my right, passing across so close in front of me that we couldn't have been more than inches apart. It swerved onto the shoulder and down into the ditch, where it tipped onto its side. Looking back, I saw the door open on the top side. Another car had stopped, and people were running down the embankment to help.

Inches. It was just inches away. You read about head-on collisions in the newspaper. On that day, I came within inches of being one of them, but I was not.

It has been said that to find a miracle, you need to be looking for one. I would add that sometimes you don't have to look very hard—it's there, right in front of you!

"Proclaiming thanksgiving aloud, and telling all Your wondrous deeds" (Psalm 26:7 ESV).

2

THE IMPOSSIBLE HAPPENS

---

*F*ather God, the more I think about You, the more amazed I am at how awesome You are. I'm lying here at six thirty in the morning, and I'm thinking about some of the amazing things You do.

I think of the Mercury convertible I had for a few months when I was nineteen and a sophomore in college. It was white with a black top and red leather upholstery. I found it and bought it from a dealer in Anoka where our family had bought cars before. I bought it unwisely. But what did I know? It was spring, I worked a couple of pretty-well-paying part-time jobs, and I was nineteen. In less than three months, I learned that it wasn't reasonable for me to try to afford to keep and maintain this car, so I sold it through a consignment dealer--but that's another story.

One sunny, late spring afternoon, I had an experience that defies explanation. I was driving south of Minneapolis with the top down, as usual. This was before freeways, and as I continued south along Nicollet Avenue, it became narrow, with one lane heading north and one lane heading south. Houses were farther apart, and the shrubbery and trees on both sides were heavily overgrown.

As I approached a crossroad, a car suddenly pulled out on my right and started straight across in front of me. All the intersection corners were blind corners, obscured by overgrown and heavy shrubbery, vines, and trees. I was about to crash in less than a second. At the speed at which I was going and with how close I was to the car I was approaching, there wasn't any time or space to stop.

Turn left, a silent voice within me said. So I turned left instantly into the left lane of the narrow cross street. Now, the laws of physics will tell you that at the speed I was moving, it is impossible to make a sharp ninety-degree turn. You will skid. Your car will roll over. And I was driving a convertible with no roll bars. Except for the windshield, there was no part of the car above the windowsills or above chest height. But the silent voice had said to turn left, and so I had—instantly—onto the narrow cross street, and I found myself traveling alongside the other car, on his left, only inches apart.

It all happened so fast that there was hardly time even to be amazed. I drove along right beside him for maybe a hundred feet before I could slow down and stop. The other driver looked at me, shocked. I looked at him. He continued on. I stopped and turned my car around.

Amazing. Also amazing that there were no cars approaching in that left lane I was driving in!

* * * *

Lord, on that sunny afternoon, You suspended the laws of physics that you had made, and You spared the life of this teenage boy—again. How can I give You thanks sufficiently?

"That my glory may sing Your praise and not be silent, O Lord my God, I will give thanks to You forever!" (Psalm 30:12 ESV).

3

LIVING ON
BORROWED TIME

*F*ather, here it is, four thirty in the morning, and
I have been lying here awake for over two hours
thinking about life experiences and about what I can
learn from thinking about them. I would not be here
right now were it not for specific acts of Your mercy and
Your grace, for Your intervention, for You having made
things happen the way they did, or for You keeping
things from happening. Without Your intervention, my
family would not exist—not my wife or our children.
Our grandchildren would not even have been born.

It all goes back to that December day many years
ago when we were moving to California. We were a
young family with two little children at the time. Our
car was a nine-year-old Chrysler, and we were pulling a

four-wheel U-Haul trailer loaded with household goods and furniture along old Route 66. We were passing through Flagstaff, Arizona, at about five thirty on a Saturday evening, approaching the last traffic light—a red light—at a wide street with traffic streaming across in both directions.

Beyond the light, the highway proceeded downhill, out of town through the mountains. It went downhill for miles and miles, curving around and between the mountains, with sheer cliffs down on one side, and up on the other side.

Suddenly, we had no brakes. We were about three-quarters of a block from the intersection. We couldn't slow down, and we were actually picking up speed as we approached the red light, with cars crossing in front of us in both directions. There was almost no time for panic. There was silence in the car. With no brakes, we were actually being pushed by a fully loaded four-wheel U-Haul trailer bigger than our car.

Then, just as we approached the intersection, suddenly the left rear corner of the car dropped, and the car dragged to a stop. Wow! I got out to look, and saw that the left rear wheel was off. The wheel was inside the fender, but it was off.

I was suddenly startled by a crash just behind me As if to emphasize what *could have* happened to us, two other cars had just collided, not thirty feet from us. The driver of the eastbound car hit his head against his windshield, and his face became bloody, streaked like a road map. I got back into our car and said to Yvonne, "Let's pray." And we did. Emergency services came and took away the injured driver in their ambulance.

I got out of our car again to decide what to do. As I did, a man dressed in coveralls came walking toward me from the sidewalk. He identified himself as a mechanic who owned a car repair shop not much more than a hundred feet from where we were standing. He said he was not normally at his shop on Saturdays, but for some reason had left his home and come to his shop just now. He examined our car and said we had a broken axle as well as failed brakes. He also said that he could make the repairs that very night, so I readily agreed.

We found a local restaurant only half a block away. When I opened the menu, the first item I noticed was a local delicacy, "scrambled brains." We didn't order it. We easily found a motel, also only about a half a block away. We stayed the night there, and were able to be on our way the next morning.

The sky was blue that next morning as we traveled west down through the mountains with brakes once again. As we rode along, I thought about what it would have been like to have been traveling downhill on that highway, out of control. I imagined our car going faster and faster, and then careening over the side. God had spared our lives that day, and we were barely even inconvenienced.

I saved a piece of the broken axle for a time, but it has disappeared through several moves. I saved it to remind myself and my family that we're always living on borrowed time. And also to remember that we're in Your care, Father.

Lord, You stepped in at just the moment we really needed You.

- You rescued us and gave us our lives back—again. We owe our lives and health to You.
- And besides that, You prompted the auto repair garage owner to leave his home and come to his shop at just that exact time!

We are grateful, and we thank You.
You did it—again!

"For He guards the course of the just, and protects the way of His faithful ones" (Proverbs 2:8 NIV).

4

HIGH DRAMA ON ICE

W inter in northern Minnesota is not to be taken lightly. First, it is looong. My younger daughter once observed that if you lived in the most southern part of the state, spring comes a month earlier and fall turns to winter a month later than in the far north. She was correct. Of course, that is a distance of more than five hundred miles, point to point, northwest to south.

Second, northern Minnesota winters can be extra cold. I remember the first winter we lived up there. The temperature was below zero degrees Fahrenheit at least part of every day the entire month of January.

Third, you can count on the fact that there will be major snowstorms from time to time. These storms masquerade under names like "Alberta clipper" or "blizzard." Sometimes it can take two or more days for the road crews to clear all the snow away from the roads and streets. Sometimes it can take even longer before all the sanding is complete. In the meantime, there can be icy stretches along a highway where someone may lose control of his or her car, with possibly disastrous results.

To be fair, there is one good thing that can be said about winter snowstorms in northern Minnesota: you can usually know about a day ahead of time when one of them will be arriving and moving through your area, so you are able to plan ahead. You can bring in provisions and settle in until the storm has passed. That is something that cannot be said about dealing with earthquakes or tornadoes.

* * * *

One afternoon in the month of March, I learned firsthand how dangerous it can be to be out. We had just experienced a major snowstorm, and the plows had been out. Most of the roads had been cleared, but there were some major icy patches on the roads and highways. You could be driving along on cleared pavement and suddenly come to an area covered with ice, so it was important to drive cautiously and more slowly to anticipate problems.

I was driving from the country to a nearby town, a distance of about fifteen miles. I had turned from the county road onto the state highway and had been driving about a couple of miles when I noticed a car coming toward me, swerving just a little bit. That car was a little bit out of control on the ice.

The highway only had one lane for eastbound traffic and one lane for westbound traffic, and that car was driving right up to the center line and starting to move into my lane. As it got within about fifty to seventy-five feet of me, I could see the driver. She was panicked. Her mouth was open, and she let go of her steering wheel, throwing both of her hands up into the air toward the ceiling.

Then suddenly, with no hands on her steering wheel, her car changed direction! It moved away from my lane toward her shoulder at my far left. As the car passed me, it went off the highway and into the ditch. I don't know what happened to that car, since with there being both eastbound and westbound traffic, I couldn't stop.

Whew!

Father, how did You move that car away from my lane? Actually, I know how You did it. It was easy for You. This was another experience of Your watchful care over me. Undeserving me. Merciful You. Again.

"Sing to Him; sing praises to Him; meditate on and talk of all His wondrous works, and devoutly praise them!" (1 Chronicles 16:9 AB)

5

OUT IN THE MIDDLE
OF NOWHERE

―――――――

*F*ive seconds out of an eight-hour journey-- a tiny,
minuscule fragment of time. It's only five seconds-
-and yet, what either happens or doesn't happen within
that five seconds can determine everything. Everything.

I was on my way across a remote country region—
mostly wilderness—going to a medical appointment. We
had recently purchased a newer minivan, and this was
the first time I had taken a long-distance trip with it.
One of my legs was in a long cast. Because of that, it was
necessary for me to travel in the second row, stretched
across both middle seats.

The driver knew the way and the destination. For
the first several hours we drove through an almost
unpopulated area, much of which had no cell phone

service, as there were almost no towers. Towers were rare and sparse in that whole part of the state. So I settled back, lying there in the second row of seats, and I guess I fell asleep.

Suddenly, I was awakened by the jumping and banging of the van, obviously off the road and heading down a steep incline. I yelled out and was hurled to the floor as the van crashed to the bottom of the slope, lurched, and came to a sudden stop.

The van was still right side up, but my head and upper body were on the floor and my lower body and legs were up. The way I was, I could not move or get out of the van. Fortunately, the driver seemed all right and was able to get the driver's door open, get out, and climb up the incline to the highway.

We had no cell phone service, but a passing car stopped to help. The people had satellite phone service, so they called for state trooper assistance from the nearest town. It seemed a long time to me, suspended almost upside down there between the seats, but they came and got my door opened and helped me out of the van. Amazingly, I seemed to be all right.

What had happened was that the driver had fallen asleep and the van had veered to the left, gone across the lane of oncoming traffic, hit the shoulder, and then crashed down the incline to the ditch. The van then veered to the right, barely missed the end of a large concrete culvert, and was then slowed down by soft grassy soil before coming to a sudden stop. If we had hit the culvert, the van would have been upended. As it was, it remained right side up.

The state trooper was very helpful. Although this all

took place on a Sunday evening, he was able to arrange for a repair garage to come the next day to tow the van, which was badly damaged. The trooper also helped us arrange to rent a car from a town about forty miles away so we could continue to our destination.

* * * *

The following morning at the Mayo Clinic, the doctors examined both of us thoroughly but found that, apart from slight bruises, we both were all right! And there was no additional injury to my leg. We learned, however, that the van was a total loss.

Father, once again You stepped in and showed Your awesomeness. Our van had traveled across the oncoming traffic lane safely. Hurtling down the incline and into the ditch, the van remained right side up! We missed crashing into the large concrete culvert by inches-- and both of us survived and were without injury! There was no cell phone service in the area, but the first car that stopped had satellite phone service.

"Because you have made the Lord your dwelling place—the Most High, who is my refuge—no evil shall be allowed to befall you … For He will command His angels concerning you to guard you in all your ways. On their hands they will bear you up, lest you strike your foot against a stone" (Psalm 91:9–12 ESV).

6

"IT'S FOR YOU"

*F*ather, I've been thinking about this: to me, when
You step into my life, as You have done dozens and
even scores of times, it is always exciting to me. And
when I think back to those instances, it is exciting to
me all over again. The main thing to me is that You did
it! I suppose I will never get used to the fact that You
care for me watchfully (1 Peter 5:7 AB), even though You
have demonstrated it to me so many times.

I think of that time when we went to California to
participate in a wedding on the Queen Mary. I experienced
an early setback in the airport when we arrived. We
were walking fast through the big LAX terminal when I
stumbled and went down on my right leg, straining and
bruising it seriously enough so that I couldn't put weight
on it. My son went and found a wheelchair, and I needed
to ride in the wheelchair the rest of the evening.

As planned, we all spent the night on the Queen Mary. In the morning, I found that I could only hobble around the room with my hands resting on a chair, on the bed, on the bathroom sink counter, and so on, as I still couldn't put any weight on my right foot or leg because the pain was so great. Getting dressed and ready for the day was a slow, arduous process for me.

I couldn't help wondering and being concerned about how I could function in the wedding ceremony, which was only a few hours away. Also, I didn't want to be a distraction.

Then, after about an hour, suddenly the pain left. It was gone! Wow! Thank You, Lord!

* * * *

The ceremony and the celebration dinner were fun and went well, and I was able to walk around. The rest of the day was spent touring the ship, following a guide. Since there was extensive walking, and to be cautious, I rode around in a wheelchair, following the suggestion of my wife.

We all spent the entire next day at Disneyland. Again, since there would be extensive walking all day— and again at the suggestion of my wife—we located a wheelchair for me to ride in. My grandsons took turns pushing me and seemed to enjoy it. Actually, it became a plus a few times when we were brought to the head of the line. On one of those occasions, they all chorused, "Thank you, Papa!"

* * * *

The next day we traveled back to Minneapolis, having had a long layover in Denver. Now it was late—about eleven thirty at night—as our plane taxied up to the gate in Minneapolis. My wife turned to me and said, "Did you arrange for a wheelchair?"

I hadn't. I couldn't explain why, but I hadn't even thought about it. *Now* I began to think about it. It was almost midnight on a Sunday night. Our plane was perhaps the last flight arriving. Virtually everything in the air terminal was shut down. I really should have had a wheelchair because our walk through the terminal would be a long one—from one corner of this large, sprawling airport to the opposite corner. But I didn't have one. My mind was a blank as to what to do.

I stepped out of the plane onto the ramp and started toward the gate. Then I noticed to my left an Asian man standing behind an empty wheelchair. I greeted him and asked him who the wheelchair was for. He looked at me. He didn't ask me who I was. He didn't ask for any information about me.

He just said three words:

"It's for you." Then he was gone.

Lord, You did it again!

"And my God shall supply all your needs according to His riches in glory in Christ Jesus" (Philippians 4:19 KJV).

PART SIX

GOD'S QUIET WHISPER AND LEARNING TO LISTEN

1

The Assignment

———————

One of the things I have learned in my life (I hope
I have learned it well) is that if I am prompted by
the Lord to do something *today*, then I am to do it *today*.

One such day took place when we were living in
northern Minnesota. It was a winter day, just two days
before Christmas, and we were preparing to drive
several hundred miles to be with family for a few days. I
awoke that morning with one thought: I must go and see
Joe before we leave on our trip. Since we were planning
to leave the next day, that meant that I must go and
see Joe that day --*today*. That morning I could think of
nothing else.

I can't recall ever in my life prior to that day having
experienced a compulsion like that—such a strong

urgency that there was something specific that I *must* do that day, without fail or delay.

I located a telephone number and called to be sure Joe and his wife, Judy, would be at home. I had never met Joe, but another member of our church had been praying for Judy for several years, and together we had driven the twenty-five miles or so to see her one time in the past. At that time, two of their grown sons had been at home, but Joe had not been there.

When I arrived at their home, Judy answered the door, and we went into the kitchen where Joe was at the kitchen table, sitting in a wheelchair. The three of us then sat around the table, visiting. I had not been aware that Joe was ill or of how ill he was—and he didn't talk about it. He did talk about fishing, and I told him that when spring arrived, I would take him to a nearby lake, and we would fish from the dock.

I knew my reason to be there that day was to talk with Joe about the Lord, salvation, and eternity. So I asked him a question. "Joe, have you reached the place in your spiritual life where, if you were to die tonight, you can say that you know for sure that you would go to heaven?" His answer was indefinite. So I asked him another question. "If you were to die and you found yourself walking up to the gate of heaven, and a big angel guarding the gate asked you, 'Why should I let you in?' what would you say?"

Joe's answer was, "I've lived a good life."

Joe's wife was standing about fifteen feet away, watching and listening to the conversation, very interested. I knew Joe's answer was not a good answer, but I sensed a wall in front of me that prevented me from continuing on the subject. So I said, "Joe, I have something out in the car that I want to give to you."

I went out and came back with a copy of the booklet "The Four Spiritual Laws/Would You Like to Know God Personally?" I said, "Joe, this could be the most important thing you read in your whole life."

As I handed it to him, he said, "Well, if it is that important, I'm going to put it right here." He stood it up between the saltshaker and the pepper shaker in the middle of the kitchen table in front of him. I knew I had done what I could, and I excused myself and left.

* * * *

About a week later, when we returned home, I received a telephone call from a friend who said he had stopped by Joe's home a few days after Christmas. He had learned from Judy that Joe had died on Christmas Eve. However, Joe had read the booklet and had become a totally changed man—a different man—and he wouldn't let go of the booklet.

Another friend and I then drove out to see Judy, and she told us the same story. Then she said, "I didn't know what had made the difference in Joe, but now I know." She too had read the booklet and responded to Jesus!

* * * *

Lord, I thank You for being so merciful. You saw to it that Joe had one last opportunity—maybe his only opportunity—to learn about Your salvation and to receive Your forgiveness and eternal life. It was just in time. And You saw to it that Judy also saw the change You had made in Joe and that she also learned and responded to You.

You gave me the opportunity to be an obedient servant—a messenger—bringing them the message just in time. All I did was to drive to their home, talk with them, and give Joe a booklet with an endorsement.

But that *was* the assignment. Your Holy Spirit did the rest!

Lord, I thank You that You appointed me for that assignment. I also thank You that You impressed me so strongly that I could not miss it and that I could think of nothing else until I had carried out the assignment.

And thank You for arranging things so that I could learn of the results—the amazing results. That was a real faith strengthener for me. It was a confirmation to me that I was indeed hearing from You and that I was indeed faithful and obedient to You.

So this was a learning experience for me—a lesson in learning to recognize when I am hearing from You.

"He guides the humble in what is right, and teaches them His way" (Psalm 25:9 NIV).

2

ANOTHER URGENT ASSIGNMENT

O ne spring Saturday morning, I awoke with a
thought: *There is a certain man I must see today.*
His name was Ted. I had met him briefly at least a
year before at a reception. Ted was a friend of a casual
acquaintance, who had introduced us. I had not seen
him since that first meeting.

I might have wondered why his name had crossed
my mind now, but I did not. There was an urgency
in my mind. *Today is the day. I must go and see him
today.* There was no question, no doubt, that this was
something I must do that day.

I had no idea where Ted lived, so I made some phone
calls to obtain his phone number. Then I called Ted
to ask if I could come out to visit him. He said that
would be fine, so I asked for directions to his home. It
turned out that he lived about thirty to thirty-five miles

southwest from me, and the route was a little complex. So I got into my car and headed out.

When I arrived, I found Ted to be friendly, outgoing, and gracious. He had a creative mind and was also knowledgeable about real estate. He talked a lot about future plans and about his grown children. He was living alone, way out in the country, in a well-maintained, well-cared-for home with land. He didn't mention anything about his health or any concerns about it, and his plans were all long-term plans, reaching several years into the future.

I knew in my heart that I was there for a reason, so I asked Ted if he would mind if I asked him a couple of questions. He agreed. I said, "Ted, would you say that you have reached the point in your spiritual experience that you could say that if you died, you know you will go to heaven?" Ted said he wasn't sure. So I asked him another question. "Ted, if you were by any chance going to die tonight and would find yourself walking up to the gate of heaven, and a big angel guarding the gate said to you, 'Why should I let you in?' what would your answer be?"

Ted wasn't really sure what a good answer would be, so I asked him if he would be interested in knowing what the Bible says is the right answer. He was interested, so we looked together at what God says in the Bible. We discussed the following:

- God is a God of love, and He loves us (John 3:16).
- Every person is sinful. We have each sinned and fallen short of God's glory, and the penalty for

sin is eternal death and separation from God (Romans 3:23 and 6:23).

- Jesus Christ is God's provision for humanity's sin. He was sinless and died to pay the penalty for our sins—that is, He died in my place and paid my fine.
- How do I "get in on it"? Each of us must individually confess that we know we are sinners and need a Savior. We must ask Jesus to come into our hearts and lives, to save us, and to be our Lord (John 1:12, Revelation 3:20, 1 John 5:9–12).
- Then, it is important to tell somebody (Romans 10:9–10).

This was all good news to Ted, and he prayed right there. It was as if the lights went on in Ted's understanding, and enthusiasm came with it, as well as a new appetite to learn more.

* * * *

A week later, I called Ted to ask about driving out to visit him again, but he said that the house was filled with family, so it wouldn't be a good day for me to come out.

Then about three days later, I was notified that Ted had died suddenly and had left instructions that he wanted me to speak at his funeral, which I did.

I learned later that Ted had told at least one person, and likely several other people, in detail about our conversation and his prayer on that Saturday.

- Lord, Thank You for seeing to it that Ted was given this opportunity to get in on the benefits of Your Son, Jesus's, death, to receive eternal life. It seemed as if this was the first time he had heard—at least the first time he understood—what he needed to do and why.
- Thank You for giving me the opportunity to be the messenger.
- The way everything worked out helped confirm to me once again that it was your voice communicating to my spirit the urgency of what to do and to "do it now."

So, this was another lesson in learning to recognize Your voice and in the absolute importance of being obedient.

"This is what the Lord says—Your Redeemer, the Holy One of Israel: 'I Am the Lord your God, Who teaches you what is best for you, Who directs you in the way you should go'" (Isaiah 48:17 NIV).

3

THE ROAD (ALMOST) NOT TAKEN

*A*merican writer Robert Frost once wrote a poem entitled "The Road Not Taken." This account is about a road that might have been one of those roads.

Sometimes a change of plans may bring about a surprising, good result that the original plan would have missed.

One afternoon, I was out driving on the county roads, delivering "Jesus" videos to the neighbors. I had obtained maps that showed all the roads in each township. I would stay on one road, driving straight ahead and stopping at each house. I would then highlight the map with a yellow marking pen to show where I had been. This system seemed simple enough, and it worked for me.

That afternoon, I was driving west on a paved road, looking ahead to a house where I would stop next. I was just approaching a point where an unpaved road to my right went north. My thought was, *I'll go up along that road on another day.* I was just about to pass that road when, out of the corner of my eye, I noticed a certain house. The house was a short distance from the intersection.

Again, my thought was, *I'll stop there when I follow that road on another day.* But then another, more overwhelming prompting, came to mind: *Go up to that house now.* I thought, *No, that would confuse my plans.*

But the prompting, though brief, persisted: *No, go to that house now.* So I did. I turned around, drove back, and turned onto that road. I went up to the house and knocked on the door.

The man who answered the door recognized me, and I him. We had met somewhere in the past, but not recently. He invited me in, and we sat, drank coffee, and talked for a little while. His wife had died, and he was now living alone.

As we talked, it occurred to me to witness to him. However, he had a reputation for having always been definitely uninterested in God, Jesus, or the Bible— especially as they related to him. Nevertheless, I brought up the subject and found him to be (surprisingly) interested. As our conversation went on, he continued to show interest, and after a short time, he prayed to receive the Lord Jesus Christ as his Savior and Lord.

* * * *

A little over a week later, my wife asked me if I remembered that man. She had crossed paths with his adult son and daughter, and they had told her that their dad had become a totally changed man. Whereas by reputation he had been cruel, harsh, and selfish, now he was totally different. Apparently they had learned from him about that afternoon, about his prayer, and about what the Lord had done in his life.

At around that time, he suffered a heart attack and was taken to the hospital. I went to see him in the hospital, and we had a very good visit. From the hospital, he was transferred to skilled care, and never did return to the house where I had visited him on that first afternoon.

Lord, You are so wise – in addition to being loving and merciful.

- You prompted me to go to that house *on that day* – even though it wasn't on the road I was canvassing that day. You knew that if I didn't, and went "some other day," I would have knocked on the door of an empty house.
- You knew that, although by reputation he was not interested in spiritual things, on that day he would be interested. You had prepared his heart.
- You even saw to it that I received feedback and confirmation from his family members – those who knew him best – about the major changes in his personality and character--evidences of the genuineness of his prayer and of the Lord transforming him.

You moved me ahead two more steps in learning to recognize and to obey your promptings.

Thank You!! Thank You!!

"My sheep hear my voice, and I know them, and they follow Me" (John 10:27 ESV).

"And your ears will hear a word behind you, saying, 'This is the way; walk in it," when you turn to the right hand and when you turn to the left" (Isaiah 30:21 AB).

4

MY ELUSIVE NEIGHBOR

---

*I*n life, if there is one thing I can expect, it is the unexpected. We have a tendency as we go through life to assume certain things, based on past experiences. However, if we are surprised often enough and regularly enough, the next surprise becomes less of a surprise. In other words, if I assume a surprise, it will be less of a surprise and more of a fulfillment of an assumption.

Early one afternoon, I was working on a project that seemed important to me at the time—a project that involved making a series of phone calls, maybe sending several e-mails, seeking to track down some information, making further plans, and following through.

Suddenly, my whole train of thought was interrupted. The name of my next-door neighbor came to my mind: George, a neighbor whom I had seen only a few very brief times in the five years we had lived here. I had taken some pastry to his house during our first Christmas here. He was almost unresponsive to that overture.

The gentle prompting in my heart and mind was that I should seek to be a witness to George. Today. *Today? Why today?* I had had fleeting thoughts more than once in the past about talking with George about spiritual things—fleeting thoughts with no sense of immediacy or urgency. *Some time*, I thought, but I had never followed through.

But now, the gentle but persistent prompting was clear: *today*.

My first thought in response was, *Well, maybe later today, after I have made some of these phone calls.* But I couldn't get away from thinking about George, and the thought, *Today.*

I began to realize that George was to be my number one priority. But how? George was really a stranger. To say that he kept to himself would be an understatement. Months could pass without even a glimpse of George. Sometimes we would speculate as to whether or not he was still actually living in that house next door. But then I would see his pickup truck parked on the street in front of his house. I might later catch a glimpse of him leaving the house, getting into the pickup, and driving away. He always seemed to be in a hurry. There was no opportunity to even shout a greeting to him.

So what do I do?

The thought came to me that I should go out onto our back patio—the patio is on the side of my house facing his yard. The property line is about fifteen to twenty feet away. *Maybe* he is at home, and *maybe* if I were to sit out there and read for a while he might eventually come outside. *Maybe* he might walk around to the side of his house, and *maybe* he might venture near the property line, where *maybe* he'll be close enough to where I was sitting that I could greet him without shouting.

If any of this were to happen, it would be for the first time, as I have spent hours and hours outside during the several years we have lived here, working on my lawn, filling our bird feeders, and so on. I had never seen George come out and walk around while I was outside. Father God, would You make all this happen today?

I went out onto the patio and began to read. I hadn't been out on the patio for much more than five minutes when George came out of his house, walked around the side and right up to the property line, where he stopped. In this entire time, he had not looked at me.

I greeted him and asked how he was. He volunteered that he was working part time but was looking for full-time work, and he briefly described what he was looking for. He named a small town in another state which was specifically where my son was located at the time! I told him that it happened that I could get him some information that could be helpful to him, available through my son, which was true.

He said he was in a hurry right now to get to his job. I asked when and where would be a good time and place to talk next. He said that the next morning at about eleven o'clock he would be at the local library, looking on one of the computers. I said fine, I would meet him there and bring some information.

Lord, it is amazing that he would talk and say so much. What a drastic change!

* * * *

The next day, I met him there at the library, and we went to a reading area where there wasn't anyone else around so that we could talk. I gave him the information about job opportunities, and we talked about that. Then I asked him a couple of questions about spiritual things, and we talked about that for a little while. On the subject of praying to receive Jesus Christ as His Lord and Savior, he asked me if that was something he could do at home, and I said yes he could. I gave him a booklet that I have found helpful. We then got together one more time the next day at the library and talked further.

The day after that, there was a "For Sale" sign in his yard, and on the following day, a "Sold" sign was added! George moved out right away and was gone.

* * * *

Father God, You knew about all this, and prompted me when You did.

- You knew He was about to list his house with a realtor,
- The house would sell right away, and
- He would move out right away and be gone.
- But you also knew that on that one day he would come outside and walk around.
- It would be at that certain time.

- You prompted me to be outside on my patio on that day, at that exact time.
- You knew George would be more open and talkative *that one time*, with the result that we could talk, then meet and talk further.

Amazing!

* * * *

As it turned out, that other project worked out without me having to make many of those anticipated phone calls, and I succeeded in getting what I was after in just a fraction of the time I had expected it to take.

"The steps of a man are directed and established by the Lord when He delights in his way [and He busies Himself with his every step]" (Psalm 37:23 AB).

5

WHO'S BEHIND THE WHITE DOOR?

---

*I*n the Christian life, we would like to know all the answers. As it is, however, we only will know what God reveals to us. We may make assumptions about other things, but it is important to remember that that is all they are—assumptions.

I experienced that one autumn afternoon while driving along a country road in northern Minnesota. I was on my way to see a friend, a retired attorney, who lived in a very well-manicured place further out in the country. As I passed the farm of a couple— Andy and Mavis—a thought came into my mind that I should stop in and see them. Mavis was a long-term Christian believer, but Andy was not. Mavis was a faithful, regular church attender; Andy was not. He would attend funerals-- that was it for him. Not only that-- he would also give Mavis a hard time about her Christian lifestyle.

The thought that came into my mind was more than a passing thought. It was not a *sometime* or a *someday*. No, it was an actual prompting of something to do *today*. As I was on my way to see someone else, I decided that I would go to see Andy and Mavis right after that. I had peace about that plan.

About an hour and a half later, I pulled up into the driveway at Andy and Mavis's house and knocked on the door. Imagine my surprise when their younger cousin, Chuck, answered the door. He told me Mavis and Andy were both away, and invited me in to have a cup of coffee.

Chuck and I knew each other, but mostly casually and indirectly. He brought me up to date on his life. He had just graduated from high school, was visiting here for about a week, and then was heading to college in another part of the state.

I knew he had been attending the youth program in a good church, so I assumed he was a believer. Imagine my surprise when at some point in the conversation he said something to the effect that you can get to heaven through just about any of the religions in the world. As it turned out, Chuck said he was not confident that he himself would get to heaven and was not sure at all what it would take for him to qualify to get in.

I asked Chuck if he would be interested if I were to show him what the Bible says about that. He said he would. After looking at several scriptures together and discussing them, he prayed in confession and surrender to the Lord, asking Him to save him. After further discussion and prayer together, we agreed to meet again before the end of the week, and I left to go home.

* * *

Father God, thank You for prompting me to go there. I am glad I was obedient. I was expecting to see Andy and Mavis. But You knew Chuck was there, and that Andy and Mavis were not, so Chuck and I could have that visit. I didn't need to know in advance; I just needed to be obedient to your prompting.

"The secret things belong to the Lord our God; but those things which are revealed belong unto us and to our children forever ..." (Deuteronomy 29:29 KJV).

6

"WE WOULD HAVE BEEN KILLED"

*T*here are some things that you just can't prepare for. They come about without prior announcement. Sudden. Unpredictable. Instantaneous. Yet requiring an on-the-spot decision. A decision which can mean life . Or death.

As I sit here, I am remembering a summer day when I was traveling home. I was driving on a two-lane highway. As we approached a crossing with another highway—a four-lane divided highway—a passenger said, "This is a four-way stop. You can go." But I felt a restraint--a need to pause.

The road was dry, and the sky was overcast. It was partially dark, between late afternoon and early evening. A haze was moving in, making it just a little difficult to see clearly. I couldn't see the stop signs for the cross traffic.

Take note, reader: from here to the end of this episode; everything took place in just a few seconds.

The passenger, sounding impatient now, shouted, "Go!" But the inner voice calmly said to me, *Wait.*

Just then, I noticed a motorcycle approaching from my right, emerging from the haze. His headlight was on. I expected him to stop. But I felt a definite restraint, a prompt to wait. *Wait for the motorcycle, to see what he is going to do.*

The motorcycle slowed and moved into its left-turn lane, but it did not stop. It gradually began to turn, but just before it turned, vehicles emerged suddenly out of the haze from both directions—*without lights*—and roared across right in front of us at top highway speeds. The one from the left was an eighteen-wheeler.

This was *not* a four-way stop!

I had thought that I had not been able to see the stop signs for the cross traffic because of the haze. The fact was, *there were no stop signs.*

After the motorcycle had turned and we had safely crossed, I looked at the passenger and said, "We would have been killed." The passenger, still stunned, just nodded.

Right now, as I sit here reliving this experience, I feel a chill on my neck and back.

Lord, thank You for the calm promptings telling me to wait. Thank You that the promptings were strong enough that I took note and heeded them.

"Who is the man who fears the Lord? Him will He instruct in the way that he should choose" (Psalm 25:12 ESV).

PART SEVEN

TIMING AND FULFILLMENT OF GOD'S PLANS

1

A SERIES OF ASTOUNDING
DEVELOPMENTS

―――――――

I received a letter from a Campus Crusade for Christ
staff member friend in California in which she said
that every day for her is an adventure because of the
unusual, unexpected ways that things happen in her
life.

I had known for some time through a continuing,
gentle, persistent witness in my heart that I had an
assignment to obtain and distribute a specific large
number of copies of a specific video portraying the life
of Jesus as presented in the Gospel of Luke. The time
came when I was strongly impressed that it was time
to get started with the project. The project involved
personally delivering a video to households within the
six townships in the area.

The very week that I was preparing to inquire about the cost per video, I received a notification in the mail informing me that, for the first time ever, the videos were to be made available for half of the previous cost! This was timely, wonderful news to me, as I had not yet talked to anyone about partnering with me to pay for the videos. Since a large number of videos was involved, this development would result in significant savings!

My next step, after further prayer, was to place some long-distance phone calls to some men whose names came to mind, asking them to partner with me in the costs. The astounding result was that I only needed to make three calls before all of the needed funds were volunteered!

The first setback resulted from an injury and necessary surgery to my left leg, which led to weakness and other problems. However, after considerable delay, the distribution began in earnest.

* * * *

Several months later, on one particular evening, I was out in a semirural area, knocking on doors and giving away videos, all without unusual incident. It was well after dark before I finished for the evening and returned home.

After I had been at home for a short while, I walked into the living room. As I turned to walk from the piano toward the couch, I suddenly collapsed to the floor with an intense pain in my left leg.

I had no idea what had just happened to my leg. What I did know was that I was in serious pain. I also knew that I could not get up from the floor, at least not for a while. I rolled to a sitting position on the floor and just sat there for a while. My wife had quickly come into the room to help. Eventually the pain lessened considerably, and I was able to get up, with much difficulty, from the floor. I still had no idea what had happened to my leg, but with a pair of crutches, I was able to move around in the house.

That night, I had plenty of time to think: whatever had happened to my leg could have happened even an hour earlier when I was miles away from home, walking in the dark from someone's house to my car. I would have found myself sitting or lying on the ground in the dark in serious pain with no one around to help.

It could have happened, but Lord, You didn't let it happen that way. You literally held it all together until I had returned home and was inside, in the safety and protection of our own home, and I thank You! Every time I think about it, I thank You again.

We obtained an appointment with the specialist at Mayo Clinic. She instantly diagnosed the condition, and I learned a new term:

Avulsion fracture. This is defined as the pulling off of sections of bone to which a muscle tendon is attached. So that is what had happened.

Surgery would be required to reattach the tendon to the bone—the surgeon called this "industrial-strength surgery"—so my leg would be in a cast for a month, which meant that I would pretty much be confined to home for all that time. That meant that the entire month of September would be lost from distributing videos—a month I had been counting on..

* * * *

While waiting for my leg to heal and following care advice, I began a search for a partner to go with me to visit the homes and farms. I asked a friend, who was able to help for about two weeks. Then I asked a pastor friend to see if he could locate any volunteers. The first man that agreed to go, it turned out, had some health problems of his own, so he couldn't be out for more than about two to three hours on any one day. Then after about two weeks, he left the state.

The next man who was recommended to me said he could only go on Saturdays, as he worked full time Monday through Friday-- so we were able to make visits on Saturday. Then, one day, he told me he would be available *every* day the very next week. It turned out that his employer, for whatever reason, had decided to shut down the entire business for that whole next week! The timing of that could not have been better. So we made good use of the time that entire next week.

To that point, we had been having good weather, but that was about to change. One day, the temperature dropped, and the entire region was hit by a major ice storm. Everything was coated with a thick covering of ice. With my walking problems, it was now impossible for me to go out and get around. What was I to do? Someone tried to encourage me, telling me that I had done the best I could. However, I knew that my assignment *wasn't* just to "do the best I can." I knew I could not stop until the project had actually been completed.

I received a long-distance call from one of my sisters-in-law. We discussed praying that the Lord would solve the ice problem. She suggested that we also ask the

Lord for a few days beyond that that would be conducive to walking outside. In response, I was surprised to hear myself say, "Let's ask the Lord for fifty days." So we did. We asked the Lord for fifty days.

So, what happened? For the next five days, the temperature got up to fifty degrees and the sun shone all day in blue skies; all the ice melted during this time, and the ground dried. Then for at least the next *fifty days*, the weather remained dry! The temperature dropped, but the weather remained dry. Lord, this is astounding! I talked about this with my sister-in-law and others. Then several years later, I brought up the subject in conversation with her and asked her if she still remembered that experience. She said yes, she certainly did!

We made good use of those fifty days. I had found another volunteer—one who worked nights--so we were able to get out in the daytime every day.. He stayed on the project with me until it was completed and every one of the videos had been given out.

One fact that made the project take longer was that during the daytime, we would find no one home at many houses. That would require that we go back, usually in the early evening or on another day. In some cases, several visits needed to be made before finally finding someone at home.

One well-meaning businessman friend suggested that I could just leave the videos in the mailboxes. However, I knew that my assignment was to personally put them in the hands of the people. Another suggested that I mail them. Again, I could not do that for the same reason. However, I began to discover that at an increasingly high percentage of homes, someone was there on our first attempt, even in the daytime!

* * * *

In conclusion: Yes, we finished distributing the videos—just about a day before a major snowstorm moved into the area. We had been warned that it was coming.

Lord, it just seems almost unbelievable the way this all worked out. All of the amazing developments along the way that made it possible—in spite of the many obstacles and roadblocks—to begin, to keep going, and to complete the assignment. Those of us who lived through it, who talked and prayed much about it along the way, and who saw these many remarkable developments will never forget.

Again, Lord, You are so amazing!

"I will ponder all Your work, and meditate on Your mighty deeds" (Psalm 77:12 ESV).

2

A CHAIN IS AS STRONG AS …

I 'm sitting here in the evening darkness, just thinking
about how little events in our lives lead to other little
events. Sometimes an event turns out to be not so little,
and sometimes one event will slide into the next in such
a way that we hardly even think about it at the time.

Think of a chain of events as a literal chain. If one
link—any one link—were missing, there would be a gap,
and the chain of progression would stop at that point.
What *would* have followed does not take place.

I think of how it came about that I met Yvonne, the
young woman who would become my wife. We did not
know any of the same people; we had no acquaintances
or friends in common. We grew up several hundred
miles apart. We did not attend any of the same schools

or colleges. We did not attend any of the same churches. And yet, there was a chain.

The First Link in the Chain

After high school, I enrolled at Northwestern in Minneapolis.

The Second Link in the Chain

During the first month, I met a fellow freshman named Ray, and we struck up a friendship. Ray was a Minneapolis boy and was into music, as I was. He invited me to his home, and I learned that the family had a piano and some recording equipment.

The Third Link in the Chain

Ray also sang, just as I did, so we found another student, formed a men's trio, and did a little singing as well as some informal recording. We also took girls out on occasional double and triple dates.

One day, after several months, Ray invited me to a meeting of the college group at the church his family attended. The group met every Friday evening. At first, I wasn't interested. I asked him what kind of church it was. He named the church; it was a Covenant church. At that point, I was not familiar at all with the Covenant denomination, and my response was, "What's a Covenant?"

Ray's answer reminds me of what Jesus's disciple, Philip, said to Nathaniel, whom he had invited to meet Jesus: "Come and see." That was Ray's answer to me; he encouraged me to come and see. I didn't go then, but Ray invited me two or three more times. I finally went.

The Fourth Link in the Chain

I found the college group at the church to be fun to be with. About twenty-five or thirty people were there; some were students at the University of Minnesota, some were students at other colleges, and some were in the working world. After the meeting, a bunch of them went bowling, and we went too. We had a good time. I came again and started to attend occasionally, along with Ray.

At some point, partway through our second year at Northwestern, Ray checked out of school and joined the army. By this time, however, I had met Howie at the Covenant church. Howie was a University of Minnesota student and was interested in golf, as I was. He and I began playing golf at least once a week. This connection helped keep me attending the Covenant church. I now knew a lot of people at the church and pretty much considered myself a regular.

Eventually, Howie "discovered" a girl that began to absorb just about all of his free time, and he no longer had much time for golf. At about this time, though, a fellow named Don, a cousin of Howie, returned home, having just finished his stint in the navy. I met him for the first time at the Covenant church, where his entire family attended regularly.

The Fifth Link in the Chain

Don and I became instant friends. We had interests in common, including golf. Also, he and I, along with eight or ten others at the church, became an informal social group, getting together at somebody's home or doing something else at least once every weekend.

The Sixth Link in the Chain

Now that he had completed his obligations in the navy, Don enrolled at the University of Minnesota.

The Seventh Link in the Chain

While attending the "U," he got involved a little bit in the Covenant Club there.

The Eighth and Ninth Links in the Chain

Sometime later down the line, Don called me and said that the "Cov Club" of the University was going to conduct a Sunday-evening Mother's Day program at a Covenant church in the Lake Minnetonka area— about twenty-five miles from Minneapolis. I had never attended any meetings of the "Cov Club," and I had never been to that church. He asked me if I would like to sing with the musical group as part of the program. I said I would, and we made plans.

... ...

The program included our music, some other features, and two speakers. One of the speakers was a pretty brunette, who caught my attention. Her name was Yvonne. After the program, with Don by my side, I approached Yvonne and introduced Don and myself to her. I learned that she was not a student at the U of M either but was in nurses' training at the Swedish Hospital School of Nursing, a highly rated hospital-based nurses' training school. She was also taking classes at Augsburg College in Minneapolis.

She had never been to this church before either, and although she was not a student at the U of M, she was well enough known by the leadership of the "Cov

Club" that she had been asked to be a speaker on the program. I didn't ask for a phone number or seek to pursue anything further.

More Links in the Chain, Coming from the Other Direction

Two weeks later, on a Sunday evening, I arrived at the large Covenant church that I had now been attending regularly for several years. The service was ready to begin, and Don and I took seats way in the back. A young women's trio stood up to sing. From where I was sitting, I couldn't see them very well. But then Don said something that grabbed my attention. The way he worded it was, "You know one of them." I looked more carefully and recognized Yvonne.

At the end of the service, I said to Don that I would like to see about arranging a double date—Yvonne with me and one of the other girls with Don. He agreed, so we went up to the front. I reintroduced myself to her, asked her for a date, and suggested my idea. She agreed, and once we started dating, that was it! There would be no one else for either of us!

* * * *

Thinking about all this, I recently wrote in my journal that "each link was vital; each led to, and was connected to, the next link." I also wrote in my journal,

Father,

About all the "chain links" that brought us together— you went to a lot of effort to make that happen. It must have been pretty important to You, and I thank You! But then, You did tell us to "Trust in the Lord with all your heart, and lean not on your own understanding. In all your ways acknowledge Him, and He will direct your paths." (Proverbs 3:5–6 NIV).

"O Lord, You have searched me and known me! You know when I sit down and when I rise up; You discern my thoughts from afar. You … are acquainted with all my ways. For You formed my inward parts; You knitted me together in my mother's womb" (Psalm 139:1–3, 13 ESV).

3

FINDING OUR
PERFECT HOUSE

S ince our move from Northern Minnesota to the southern part of the state, hardly a week went by without one of us remarking to the other about the house we found and about how it suits us in every way and meets our needs.

When the time came for us to begin thinking about retiring, there were several questions to consider. I estimated that I was within a year to a year and a half from completing some long-range assignments and projects. We also, after prayer and consideration, decided that the right location to move to would be a little town in the southern part of the state. We had a daughter who lived in the area with her family, and I was already occasionally commuting to the Mayo Clinic.

So the search began for a suitable house for us. We made contact with a real estate agent who turned out to be just the right one. My wife's schedule was more flexible than mine, so she would drive to our daughter's place, stay a couple of days, help out there, and go on the search for houses. The realtor would always have several listings in mind, so they would go and look at each one. After looking at them all, she would call me and then would drive back to our home in the north the next day. When she returned home, we would look at the pictures and the listing information together and discuss each one. From time to time, the two of us would go south and look at the ones that were at the top of our list.

* * * *

Time went by, and many houses "crossed our screen," but none of them seemed right for us. Although a great many houses came and went from the market, nearly all seemed to be much older than we were really looking for. With some, the price was much higher than we were prepared to pay. It seemed that all were built so there was a lot of stair climbing required. Some had water problems in the basement.

We owned a baby grand piano, and Yvonne would look for the floor plan of a living room that was shaped or designed to accommodate the piano. Many of the houses were not laid out that way.

* * * *

Eventually, we were approaching crunch time, and we had not found a house that would meet our needs. By this time, Yvonne estimated that she had looked at approximately one hundred houses, and I had looked at about twenty or twenty-five of those. But the search went on.

Then, just when we were reaching a critical point, the realtor told us that a certain house had just come onto the market that we "just have to see." Yvonne went to see it and called me right away.

"Bill, you just have to come and see this house."

So, I went down to look at it. When we drove up to the front of the house, I was immediately struck by the attractiveness of the outside. We went in and toured every room. We could see that everything about the house was exactly what we had envisioned living in. We liked the moderate size of the house and the floor plan. Everything was on one level, with no steps up or down. The design was bright, airy, and cheerful. Its construction was recent—about ten to twelve years old. The price was within reason. And it was even handicap-accessible, which is something we hadn't really thought about, but which was a definite bonus!

When we signed in the realtors' ledger on the kitchen counter, I noticed that only one other person had been to see it ahead of us. So we began the process. We made an offer, entered into negotiation, and went through the inspection, escrow, and closing.

During the process, we learned that the house had been vacant for more than a year. During that time, the owners had made absolutely no effort to sell it. They merely used it to house members of their family who were visiting from the east coast or some other distant place. The owners had just now decided to list the house on the market—just now, when we were at the point where we were ready to buy it!

So Lord, You really saved this house for us. You saved it until it was just the right time for us, so that we would find it and purchase it. Thank You! Thank You!

"And my God will supply every need of yours according to His riches in glory in Christ Jesus. To our God and Father be glory forever and ever. Amen." (Philippians 4:19–20 ESV)

"Come and listen, all you who fear God; let me tell you what He has done for me" (Psalm 66:16 NIV).

4

WHEN PATHS CROSS

"C rossing paths"—an expression that immediately paints a picture of an intersection. Two paths—long or short, straight or crooked—that meet and cross at some point and then go on.

Picture two people, each on his or her respective path. One's path consists of several events during the day. There may be either a sequence or a planned order. Unbeknownst to one person, at some point in the day, his or her path will cross that of the other.

At the same time, the other person is following his or her own list or series of events or tasks, which together constitute his or her path.

If this is part of a movie plot, the suspense builds, as we all wonder if the two parties will reach that intersection at the same time. If they don't, they will not meet. A minute's delay here or there will make all the difference. If one incident is left out, that will change the timing.

I crossed paths a few years ago with someone in California through a very tenuous string of incidents. There was only a ten-minute window in which we could have met. The significance of that meeting will become clear later on.

The adventure began when my wife and I traveled to California to meet our son and his family. Without our prior knowledge, he had booked our entire party into the Disneyland Hotel for the following night. Thus began the path.

While we were checking in, I learned that there was a grand piano in the lobby. Playing the piano is something I do; I seek out and play them whenever I find a grand piano in a hotel lobby, a restaurant, a cruise ship, and so on. However, the Disneyland Hotel is really three separate hotel buildings, and I learned that the piano was in one of the other two buildings. So this was step two along the path.

The next day, we all went into the Disneyland park, and then enjoyed dinner and the evening fireworks. Immediately after the fireworks, we returned to our hotel. Step three. Now the clock was ticking.

When we arrived back at our room, we found that the card key would not at first open the room door, but after some delay, another member of our family arrived with a key that did unlock the door. The delay became step four. Tick-tock.

I called the front desk, which was in the Marina Tower, to tell the clerk about the problem and set out to go there for a new replacement key. When I stepped out of the elevator in our building, I looked for the piano, but could not find it. Step five. The minutes were passing.

Just as I was leaving the building, a member of the hotel supervisorial staff came around the corner. She knew about the piano. Incidentally, she said that she was not normally there at that time but for some reason had come in that night. I went with her as she looked for the piano, but we did not find it. Then she recalled that it had been moved to the third building, the Sierra Tower, to a guest lobby area near the elevators. Step six. The minute hand was crawling forward.

I left to go to the Marina Tower to get a card key, but planned to stop at the Sierra Tower for just a few minutes at the piano. However, I found that, because of construction and remodeling in progress, the entrances facing the main sidewalk were boarded up with plywood, which would require me to go halfway around the building to be able to enter. So I decided to go on to the Marina Tower first and then stop at the Sierra Tower on my way back. Step seven. Again, tick-tock.

I received the replacement key and returned to the Sierra Tower. I went in through the side entrance and found the piano—a beautiful six-foot grand—where the staff lady had told me it would be. However, the piano was all closed up and appeared to be locked. If it truly was locked—and I could see that the lock was locked—I, of course, would have simply left.

However, for some reason, I nevertheless took hold of the lid and tried to lift it. To my surprise, it lifted easily! I could see then that though the lock was indeed locked, the person who had locked it had not quite pushed the lid down enough to engage the lock. Step eight. The second hand was rounding the top.

So I sat down and began to play a gospel tune. I

was not expecting anyone to enter that area. I did not anticipate anyone walking in. It had not occurred to me that anyone would come in there. I had expected to be alone at the piano. But I was only part way through the first song when a young lady emerged from the hall, walked through the doorway to a large couch about eight feet from the piano, sat down, and appeared to begin meditating or praying. She did not look at me at all. Step nine.

I finished the song and then began another gospel song. As I finished that song, she looked at me, so I asked her if she recognized that song. She said no. I asked if she had recognized the one before it. She said no; she hadn't recognized that one, either. We began a brief conversation, in which she said she had grown up in the church but had now walked away and no longer believed any of it. I told her a little bit of my story of faith, but this was not a time for a long conversation. So we agreed that I would send her an e-mail with my story. As I left, she again said she would look forward to reading my story.

The next week, now back at home, I composed a lengthy e-mail containing my story and an appeal for her to put her faith and trust in Jesus Christ. (I have included that e-mail in the appendix at the back of this book.) As I did, I thought about the string of events and incidents that had led to that meeting that evening—that crossing of paths. Each step was important and led to the next, and the precise amount of time for each had led me to be at the piano for that exact ten minutes when our two paths would cross and that conversation about vital gospel truths could take place.

Lord, You had this all worked out and timed. I pray again now that she will respond to You and that You, O Father, will draw her to Yourself in Jesus's holy name.

"For every purpose and matter has its right time" (Ecclesiastes 8:6 AB).

"So teach us to number our days, so we may get us a heart of wisdom" (Psalm 90:12 AB).

5

BLACK FRIDAY IN MINSK

*H*ow do you communicate if you find yourself surrounded only by people who do not speak your language and you do not speak theirs?

In 1986, one of the waning years of the USSR, I traveled there as a participant in a human-rights project. One reason that I participated was that this provided a way for me to go to the Soviet Union. My reason was that I was looking for opportunities to be a witness to people over there, and I learned that there would be a good deal of free time while there. So armed with a plan, I joined in and went.

On one particular day, we were in Minsk, the capital city of Belarus. Belarus, more commonly known in the West as "White Russia," is bordered by Russia on its northeast, the Ukraine on its south, Poland on its west, and Lithuania and Latvia on its northwest. The area around the city of Minsk is largely flat with some rolling hills. With no natural protection provided by the terrain, Minsk is vulnerable to invading forces. As a result, the city has been leveled to the ground six times in its history by invading armies.

So here I was in the city of Minsk, on this beautiful day in the month of June, looking for someone to talk with.

Historically, the dominant language of the people of Minsk and of the republic as a whole is Belarusian—a language definitely influenced by and yet distinct from that of Poland, the neighbor to the west. Having been under Soviet control for seven decades by that time, Russian had become the second dominant language of the people. English-speaking people were rare in Minsk. However, my group was staying in a large hotel there in the city, and I did find one person who spoke English fluently—one of the desk clerks.

That afternoon, as I approached the hotel registration desk, I noticed that the entire lobby—a very large lobby—was quiet, almost deserted, so I took the opportunity to begin a conversation with the desk clerk about Jesus Christ. I was wearing a lapel pin, which someone had given me just before I left New York City. The lapel pin was a cross, and that became the focus of our conversation.

During our conversation, no one—not even one person—entered through any of the doors to the large lobby of that large hotel. But within ten seconds of the conclusion of our conversation, the doors literally burst open, and many people rushed in and headed directly to the registration desk where we were standing. The scene resembled Black Friday at any one of many major department stores in the United States—the morning after Thanksgiving, when the doors are first unlocked and the hordes of frantic customers practically smash their way in to scoop up the bargains.

Timing.

Father God, it was almost as if you locked all the doors to that hotel lobby on that afternoon in Minsk and kept them locked through our entire conversation. Then, when we were finished, You opened the doors. Again, amazing! You do what it takes to get the job done, don't You, Lord?

"You have multiplied, O Lord my God, Your wondrous deeds and Your thoughts toward us; none can compare with You! I will proclaim and tell of them, yet they are more than can be told" (Psalm 40:5 ESV).

Appendix A

The Dream:
Missing the Train

O ne summer night on the farm, when I was
between the seventh and eighth grades, I went
to bed as usual, without any special concerns that I
recall. However, late into the night, I had a dream that
greatly disturbed me. In the dream, Jesus came to take
with Him His children—the believers, the redeemed,
the saints, the saved ones. This was the Rapture. In my
dream, however, it was not a matter of going up into the
sky. Rather, Jesus arrived with a passenger train. The
saints began to run toward the train from all directions.

I also began to run toward the train. I was some
distance away at the start, but I ran and kept running
toward the train. Soon the train began to move, very
slowly at first. In my dream, the train was facing toward
my right and began to move toward my right. Now I was
closer, and as I ran, all of the people ahead of me were
scrambling onto the slowly moving train. But the train

was beginning to move a little bit faster and a little bit faster still.

I was getting closer now and was about fifty yards away. Most of the people had now boarded, so there were only a few of us still running to board the moving train. My last thirty yards or so were up a slight incline, and the train was increasing in speed.

Now I was within fifteen or twenty feet of the train, but it was moving a little faster than I could run. The last car, like an observation car, was in front of me, moving fast.

I ran with my last burst of desperate, frantic energy to try to at least grab for a railing on the side of that last car of the now fast-moving train, but I couldn't quite reach it. I couldn't reach it in time.

The train was gone. I had missed it. I had missed the Rapture. This twelve-year-old boy had missed the Rapture. I stood alone beside the railroad tracks, watching as the train disappeared into the distance.

Then I awoke from the dream to a sunshiny summer morning. But it was quiet. Totally quiet. Too quiet.

My mother--Where was my mother? Had the Rapture taken place? I knew Dad would have left for work early in the morning, but Mom would be here. Where was she? Did she go with Jesus in the Rapture? Without me? Am I here, left behind? Is she gone? I had to find her! I got up and looked all around in the house. I checked every room. It was all quiet. She wasn't anywhere in the house.

Even more frantic now, I ran outside to see if she was out there—somewhere. I looked for her. I called for her.

Then I found her out in the garden on the other side of the barn. She was so calm. So was I—now that I knew she was still here. I was not alone! I had not been left behind!

I was so relieved. Mom was not gone, the Rapture had not taken place, and I had not missed it. But I have never forgotten the dream-- and every time I think of it, emotions well up in me all over again.

"Therefore, you also must be ready, for the Son of Man is coming at an hour you do not expect" (Matthew 24:44 ESV).

Appendix B

The E-mail

Hi _____,

It was really great meeting you at the Disneyland Hotel. I promised to send you a summary of my journey and discoveries.

On my way to one undergraduate degree and two graduate degrees, I found that I had many questions. I *had* to know the answers, so I went on a quest for information and evidence. Here are some things I discovered in my search, that made a big impact on my life:

I met a young man in the student union at Kansas State University, who had been a devout Buddhist. He told me he had studied Buddhism thoroughly to find God, but had not found God in Buddhism. Now he had come to America to find God, and he had now found Him through Jesus Christ. As result, his life was transformed.

I learned of a man from India by the name of Ravi Zacharias, who found the reality of forgiveness and eternal life through Jesus Christ. Now he has dedicated his life to telling others, and he travels the world, speaking, debating, and conducting question and answer sessions on major university campuses across America and around the world. He presents the validity, reasonableness, authenticity, and reality of Jesus Christ and the Christian faith. He has written several books on the subject as well, and also appears on television from time to time. I listened to a tape of one of his appearances at Harvard University, where he fielded questions from a large audience of students and faculty. Zacharias is an extremely brilliant, articulate, well-educated man who has much of value to say—and what he has to say really makes sense. If he comes to your area, be sure to go see and hear him.

I studied the Bible itself, as well as documentation about the Bible. One of the things that impressed me was that much of the Bible is prophecy. So I checked out many of the prophecies to see what came of them. In the Bible, the criteria for a true prophet is that his prophecies must be fulfilled 100 per cent, or he is not a true prophet. I found many, many prophecies there that were specific and detailed and that were later fulfilled, as confirmed by historical records and archeological discoveries.

I am aware that there are still skeptics around, writing and teaching from the basis of the outdated writings of other skeptics from over fifty to more than a hundred years ago. However, many, many archeological and other discoveries in the last thirty to sixty years support and corroborate what the Bible says and confirm that the Old Testament and New Testament documents are genuine--and that the writers who wrote as eyewitnesses truly were eyewitnesses to Jesus's life, teaching, miracles, death, and resurrection, as they said they were.

Numerous other prophecies also predicted events that later happened, down to the last detail, including the coming of the Messiah, Jesus Christ. One prophecy, written hundreds of years before His birth, even named the community of Bethlehem as the place where Jesus would be born!

I read the writings of leading historians and legal authorities, who declared that the death and resurrection of Jesus Christ are proved "by better and fuller evidence of every sort" as substantiated events in history. C. S. Lewis, a professor at Oxford University widely acknowledged as one of the most brilliant minds of the twentieth century, described in his autobiography, *Surprised by Joy*, his journey from atheism to agnosticism and then to belief and faith in Jesus Christ as God the Son and as his Savior.

Jesus Christ is the only one who offers forgiveness and pardon, peace with God, and eternal life, because "the wages of sin is death, but the gift of God is eternal life through Jesus Christ our Lord" (Romans 6:23). Jesus said, "For God so loved the world that He gave His only-begotten Son, that whosoever believes in Him should not perish, but will have everlasting life" (John 3:16). He also said, "I am the Door; by Me, if anyone enters in, he shall be saved" (John 10:9). And He declared, "I am the Way, the Truth and the Life; no one comes to the Father but through Me" (John 14:6).

Jesus asks for a response. Revelation 3:20 says, "Behold, I stand at the door and knock. If anyone hears My voice and opens the door, I will come into him, and have fellowship with him." This is an individual invitation. And as John 1:12 says, "As many as received Him, to them He gave the power [right, privilege] to become the children of God—to them that believed on His Name."

I know of one person who began his response, "God, if You exist, I want to know You." My response to the Lord was something like this:

Lord Jesus, I need You. I admit to You that in my life I fall way short. I ask you to forgive my sins, to save me and come into my life. Help me to live for you. Thank you for dying for me, in my place.

Does a prayer similar to that express the desire of your heart? If it does, I suggest that you pray it. Christ will save you and come into your life, just as He said He would.

Let me know how things are going.

Your friend,

Bill Fisher

CPSIA information can be obtained at www.ICGtesting.com
Printed in the USA
LVOW07*0806241115

463516LV00004B/5/P